Guide to
Home Repair
and Improvement

True Value®
Guide to
Home Repair
and Improvement

by JACK MAGUIRE

illustrated by JESSICA WOLK STANLEY

Produced by The Stonesong Press and
Alison Brown Cerier Book Development
A Dell Trade Paperback

A DELL TRADE PAPERBACK

Published by
Dell Publishing
a division of
Random House, Inc.
1540 Broadway
New York, New York 10036

Cover photo copyright @ 2000 by Will Ryan
Cover design by John D. Sparks
Copyright © 2000 by The Stonesong Press, Inc., and
Alison Brown Cerier Book Development

Dell books may be purchased for business or promotional use
or for special sales. For information please write to:
Special Markets Department, Random House, Inc.,
1540 Broadway, New York, New York 10036.

DTP and the colophon are trademarks of Random House, Inc.

Library of Congress Cataloging in Publication Data
Maguire, Jack, 1945–
    True Value guide to home repair and improvement / by Jack Maguire:
    illustrated by Jessica Wolk Stanley.
ISBN: 0-440-50886-X
1. Dwellings—Maintenance and repair—Amateurs' manuals. I. Title.

TH4817.3.M32 2000
643'.7—dc21   99-045820

Printed in the United States of America
Published simultaneously in Canada
February 2000
10 9 8 7 6 5 4 3 2
RRD

Contents

How to Use This Book

The neighborhood hardware store has long been a wonderland for resourceful, do-it-yourself Americans. People who stroll the aisles inevitably wind up saying to themselves: "What could *this* be used for?" "So *that's* how it's done!" Or "I bet *I* can do that!"

Then they bring their questions to their favorite hardware guru—that man or woman whom they haven't managed to stump yet, even with the toughest questions. Every day, in neighborhood hardware stores across the country, the pros who stand behind the counter give practical answers to countless questions such as: "Can I use latex paint over an oil base?"; "How can I remove a screw when the slot is worn away?"; "What should I do about a leaky pipe when the plumber can't come until next week?"; "How do I get a wine stain out of the carpet?"; "How do I stop my radiator from knocking?"

Almost 6,000 of those neighborhood hardware stores are part of the Cotter & Company family, owner of the trademark rights for the famous True Value® name. There are True Value stores in all 50 states, plus 300 stores in Canada and stores in nearly 50 other countries. Focusing on the do-it-yourself consumer, the stores sell hardware and related products. Each local store is owned by an independent business person. Together, the stores form a co-op that owns their wholesale distributor. In July 1997, Cotter & Company merged with ServiStar Coast to Coast to form TruServ Corporation, the biggest hardware wholesaler in the $141-billion do-it-yourself industry—twice the size of its nearest competitor. TruServ Corporation is the successor to Cotter & Company's rights to the True Value trademark.

At TruServ, we decided to put the answers to the most common questions about home repairs and maintenance between covers so that you can find good advice not just around the corner but also on that dusty shelf above your workbench.

When creating this book, TruServ asked its hardware-store owners for the "golden nuggets" they love to pass along to their customers and the tips their customers have passed along to *them*. The book includes out-of-the-ordinary, downright helpful tips as well as tried-and-true instructions for the most common household repairs, improvements, and emergencies from both sources.

The book begins with a buying guide for basic tools and supplies. It then outlines a month-by-month program you can follow to take care of your home and yard. The remainder of the book provides useful, easy-to-access information and tips on floors, painting, wallpapering, ceilings, walls, windows, plumbing, electricity, heating and cooling systems, exterior features and surfaces, and lawns and gardens. The book ends with appendixes that provide a comprehensive guide for removing common stains; a glossary to help you make sense of jargon, buzzwords, and technical terms; charts and calculations for all your home repair projects; and a list of organizations and services for additional help.

To get the most from this book, the following steps are recommended:

1. First, browse through it and see all that it has to offer, so you'll know where to turn when a particular need or opportunity comes up.

2. Read about tools in Chapter 1, browse through the planning calendar in Chapter 2, and study the emergency sections at the beginnings of the other chapters. These parts provide information that is especially important for everyone to know.

3. As you read and use the book, make notes about your particular needs, accomplishments, insights, and questions.

4. From time to time, browse through the book to see what catches your eye at the moment. As any handyperson knows, different times bring different interests!

The goal of the *True Value Guide to Home Repair and Improvement* is to help you do repair and maintenance tasks effectively and comfortably, handle emergencies confidently and skillfully, and determine accurately which tasks you can do on your own and which require the assistance of a professional. Its larger purpose, however, is to encourage you to have a richer, more rewarding dialogue with your hardware-store dealer and with all the people you meet who take pride and pleasure in caring for their homes. May it serve you well!

1 The Right Stuff to Do the Job Right
Basic Tools and Supplies

This chapter answers the often-asked question "Which tools do I need the most?" Here's the low-down on the tools you'll count on again and again, and the features to look for when buying them. Once you have them, these tools will take care of the most common household repairs, maintenance tasks, home improvements, and emergencies. Special tools for painting and wallpapering, plumbing, and repairing your electrical system are described in the related chapters.

The most important *general* rule when choosing among several brands or types of a tool is to pick the one with the highest quality you can reasonably afford. A cheap tool will break and wear out faster. You'll have to replace it, and of course it'll break just when you need it most. A broken tool can even contribute to an accident.

True Value Tip

SAFETY FIRST

- Use tools only for their intended purposes and read all the directions that come with them so you use them safely.
- Store all tools where they can't be reached by young children, and when you're working with tools, keep young children away from the area (not just because of the obvious large dangers like sharp tools but also because work areas can have hazards like a nail on the floor, fumes in the air, or flying wood chips). Teach older children and teens how to use tools safely and supervise them.
- Wear goggles whenever doing work that might cause an eye injury: for example, while sawing, drilling, or sanding. Choose goggles that feel comfortable, fit snugly all around the eye area, and allow full vision.
- Wear gloves to perform tasks that are very messy, that might injure your hands, or that require a tight grip. Standard utility gloves (cotton or cotton-mix), which are sold in hardware stores, are versatile and easy to clean.
- Don't wear loose-fitting clothes or jewelry while working with tools.
- Briefly inspect tools before use to make sure that they're not damaged, that blades aren't dull, that parts aren't loose, and, in the case of power tools, that cords aren't frayed.
- Before adjusting or servicing power tools, be sure to unplug them. Also, don't leave them plugged in between tasks.
- Wear a filter mask over your nose and mouth when the task involves a lot of dust or small-particle debris (for example, plaster dust, sawdust, insulation fiber, or cement).

HAMMERS, NAILS, AND NAIL SETS

■ The most basic tool of all is a **curved claw hammer** to drive and pull out nails, tacks, and other fasteners. For maximum versatility and effectiveness, many people prefer a 16-ounce hammer (which refers to the weight of the head). If a hammer of that weight seems too heavy or unwieldy in your hand, buy at least a 12- to 13-ounce hammer. You want some mass-related power. When hefting a hammer in the store to get a feel for the most comfortable weight, keep in mind that for some tasks, you'll be hammering for a long time. A hammer that seems a little heavy in the beginning will feel *really* heavy near the end! A solid hammer typically features a forged steel head that's fitted strongly onto a hickory handle with a square, deep-wedged socket. Heavier (20-ounce), all-metal hammers, known as ripping hammers, are certainly stronger but are not as effective as claw hammers at pulling out nails or performing general home maintenance and repair tasks. They're used for heavy construction jobs like prying apart boards and nailing planks into beams or studs.

■ Buy boxes of different kinds of **nails** to suit the various tasks you anticipate. A good starting inventory is one pint-size box each of 6d, 8d, and 10d common nails ("d" means "penny," the size of the nail).

■ You should also have two or three sizes of **nail sets**. The best deal is a package of three different sizes. A nail set is positioned on top of a nail and hammered to drive the nail into the wood. This

protects the wood and allows you to drive the nail slightly below the surface. Nail sets work better than using another nail for the same purpose; it's too easy to slip and put another hole in the wood.

NAIL TYPES AND SIZES

The length of nails is measured in a unit called "penny," which is expressed in shorthand as "d." An 8-penny or 8d nail, for example, is 2½ inches long.

COMMON OR BOX NAILS: for simple maintenance and repair tasks; not much holding power

FINISHING NAILS: for exterior and interior trim or paneling; small heads that can more easily be driven below the surface and covered with putty

BARBED NAILS: for maintenance and repair tasks in which you want more holding power

ANNULAR THREADED NAILS: for plywood and drywall

SPIRAL NAILS: for hardwoods such as flooring; the nail turns as it's driven into the wood

Nail size	Length in inches
2d	1
3d	1¼
4d	1½
5d	1¾
6d	2
7d	2¼
8d	2½
9d	2¾
10d	3
12d	3¼
16d	3½
20d	4

COMMON NAIL

FINISHING NAIL

BARBED NAIL

ANNULAR THREADED NAIL

SPIRAL NAIL

SURE, YOU'VE BEEN HAMMERING IN NAILS SINCE YOU WERE FIVE, BUT HERE'S HOW TO DO IT RIGHT

To hammer safely, effectively, and comfortably:
■ Grip the handle firmly near the end.
■ Swing your strike as much as possible from the shoulder *and* elbow rather than from the wrist or the elbow alone.

■ Before driving a nail into wood, hold it in place and tap it until it stands by itself.

■ If you're worried about splitting thin or narrow wood with a nail, first make sure you're using the right type of nail (*see* Nail Types and Sizes, page 13), then gently tap it once or twice against a hard surface like concrete or scrap metal; a slightly blunted nail is less likely to cause a split.

■ To pull out a nail with the claw of your hammer without damaging the wood, first gently pry the nail a short distance out of the wood. Then slip a heavy cloth or piece of wood under the claw before pulling the nail the rest of the way out. You can also buy special claws for tough jobs.

SCREWDRIVERS AND SCREWS

■ You should have **two sets of screwdrivers**, each with a small, large, and stubby length: one set with a Phillips (cross-tipped) blade, the other with a slotted (straight) blade. The longer the blade or fatter the handle, the more power the screwdriver has. The stubby size has an extra-fat handle to compensate for the short blade; it's used when the working space is tight. A fluted screwdriver handle makes for a tight-enough grip, but even better is a slightly larger, smooth handle with a rubber covering. The blade should be well-tempered and ground. A screwdriver is well-balanced if the point where you can balance the screwdriver on your finger is very near the place where the handle and the blade meet. If you want to test a screwdriver in a set but you can't remove it without damaging the packaging, look around for the same model being sold individually or consult the dealer.

■ Instead of two sets of screwdrivers, you can buy a **ratchet screwdriver** that comes with several sizes of add-on tips of both types, and, in some models, drill bits as well. Often the tips and bits are stored in the wooden handle, which screws off and on. When you push on the handle, the head of the ratchet automatically turns the inserted tip or bit. Ratchet screwdrivers come in a wide variety of models that are equally effective, so check with your dealer about the particular model that will best suit your needs. One feature you definitely want is an automatic return. Also, be sure to test-fit the accompanying tips and bits before buying it.

■ A third option, one that many people choose today for its speed, is a **cordless power screwdriver with a rechargeable battery**. It has tips of both types and many sizes and is very handy.

■ Keep a small supply of **screws** on hand for general purposes. Buy five to ten screws in each of several different sizes, heads (flat or rounded), and tips (pointed or flat), or buy a pint-size jar or box of assorted screws.

True Value Tip

SCREWDRIVER SECRETS

■ To avoid hurting the surface you're working on, the screw, or yourself, it's important to use the right size and type of screwdriver for the job. Match the kind and size of blade tip to the screw. Before driving the screw into wood, create a small pilot hole with a nail or drill bit. Finally, for good leverage and force, push into the screw as you turn it.

■ Pismo Bob Pringle, owner of the True Value hardware store in Pismo Beach, California, passes along this tip whenever he sells a screwdriver: Rub beeswax onto the tip so screws will stick to it. This trick is especially helpful for brass or stainless steel screws, because they can't be held with a magnetic driver.

■ To remove a screw that has a worn-down slot, first try rubbing chalk on the tip of the screwdriver; this may add just enough traction that the screwdriver can turn the screw without it slipping out. If that doesn't work, put a center punch into the slot, slightly right of center and at an angle, so that when you tap the punch with a hammer, the screw will start moving counterclockwise. As soon as it's fairly loose, try turning it again with a screwdriver or even a pair of locking pliers.

GETTING ADVICE AT YOUR HARDWARE STORE

True Value Tip

Hardware store owners offer these tips to help you talk about repair strategies at your hardware store. These ideas can also cut down on the trips back and forth to the store.

■ When you go to the hardware store, bring any old parts you've removed and as much information as you can write down about the problem. A sketch can be worth a thousand words.

■ If the dealer recommends a repair strategy, make sure you know which tools you should use. Ask what might go wrong during the repair, and if it does, what to do. Don't hesitate to ask questions about anything you don't understand.

■ After you buy a package with parts inside, open the package carefully to make sure that all the parts are there before leaving the store. If you have any concerns, ask right away. If you don't open a package until you're home, do so carefully in case the contents need to be returned in the package.

■ Always keep old parts on hand until after the repair is finished. It may turn out that the only way to make a successful repair is to somehow reuse the old parts.

CARING FOR TOOLS WITH WOODEN HANDLES

True Value Tip

■ To prolong the life of the wooden handle on a hammer or other tool, from time to time thinly coat it with linseed oil, lemon oil, or even olive oil. Before using the tool again, let the oil soak into the wood until the handle feels dry to the grip, usually less than an hour.

■ When other people borrow a tool with a wooden handle, or when you're going to be using it while working with others, identify it as yours by branding it with your initials. Sara Borden learned the following trick from her True Value dealer: First, paint your initials in fingernail polish on the handle, ideally on a place you won't grip when you use the tool. Then set a match to the wet polish and let it burn itself away. The result will be permanent charred initials that look nice and do no harm to the tool. For deeper initials, repeat the process.

PLIERS AND WRENCHES

■ A pair of 8-inch **slip-joint pliers** has many uses. Their primary purpose is to fasten or unfasten nuts, bolts, and lag bolts (big, fat screws). They also work like tweezers to remove small nails or tacks. You want pliers that are made of forged steel (usually printed on the handle) with a chrome-plated exterior surface. The jaws should be machine-milled (if it's not printed on the handle, ask your dealer) and should close smoothly and firmly on a piece of wood (test it in the store). The arms shouldn't wobble away from each other when the joint is closed and you attempt to wiggle them in different directions.

SLIP-JOINT PLIERS

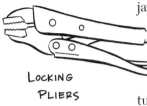

LOCKING
PLIERS

■ Also useful is a pair of **locking pliers**, often called by the brand name Vise-Grips®. After the jaws are set in place, you squeeze the handles to clamp them together. Locking pliers are used to free tight nuts and bolts. When the jaws are locked, they work like a clamp that keeps a nut in place as you turn a bolt.

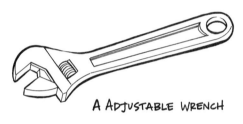

A ADJUSTABLE WRENCH

■ Also get a 10-inch **adjustable wrench** (also known as a crescent wrench) to fasten or unfasten most big nuts, bolts, and lag screws. An adjustable wrench also serves as a good holding clamp. Test any wrench you're considering buying to make sure the worm gear is tight (not wobbly) and operates smoothly.

DRILLS AND BITS

■ One of the handiest tools around the house is a **rotary power drill**. It will drill holes and drive in screws far more easily, quickly, and effectively than a hand drill or screwdriver. The simplest, most versatile model is a cordless drill with a rechargeable battery. Look for a drill that has variable speeds, a reverse switch, and a maximum chuck capacity of ⅜ inch (a larger drill isn't necessary for general maintenance and repair). Drills typically come with a variety of drill bits and screwdriver ends. A magnetized attachment will hold screws well.

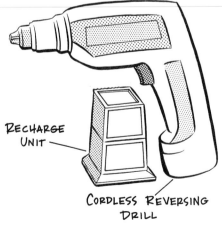

RECHARGE
UNIT

CORDLESS REVERSING
DRILL

■ If you prefer a nonelectric drill, or if you want a backup, get a **hand drill** (also called an eggbeater drill) with assorted drill bits. This is a basic and simple drill that will make holes up to ¼ inch across.

MEASURING TOOLS

■ Everybody needs a **flexible steel tape measure**. Look for a model with a lock button to hold the pulled-out tape in place. Lengths vary from 3 to 33 feet; a 25-foot one is a good choice.

■ For drawing straight lines, get a 1-foot **ruler** and an aluminum **yardstick**.

■ It is also good to have a 24-inch **carpenter's level** with at least two bubbles: one to test horizontal level and another to test vertical plumb. Try it out in the store on known level and plumb surfaces to make sure that you can read it and that it works well. Whether to get an aluminum, brass, magnesium, plastic, or wooden level depends on your own personal preference and what you want to spend. Any type works fine for general purposes.

True Value Tip

MADE-TO-MEASURE MEASURING TAPE

You can customize your flexible steel measuring tape when you're going to be making a lot of cuts. Put some masking tape on the casing, then write all the measurements for the project on hand on the masking tape. That way, you've got them right where you need them, rather than fooling around with a separate piece of paper.

True Value Tip

GOING VERTICAL

Contractors know how to measure the height of a wall without a ladder or a helper. Put the end of the tape rule on the floor next to the wall. Pull out about 4 feet of tape. With one hand, hold the tape firmly against the wall at chest height. With your other hand, keep feeding out more tape, 1 or 2 feet at a time, until you reach the ceiling or another high place you want to measure.

*True
Value
Tip*

CLEAN CUTS

Sawing through plywood can easily leave a splintery, ragged edge. To keep this from happening, apply a strip of masking tape to the surface you intend to cut, draw your line on top of the tape, and saw right through the tape *and* the plywood. When you're finished, peel away the tape and admire the clean cut.

SAWS

■ To saw wood, get a **handsaw** designated as "general purpose." It cuts either along or against the grain, while a cross-cut saw is made just for cutting across the grain. Saws are classified according to the number of teeth per inch (tpi). Look for a mid-range model: 8, 9, or 10 tpi. The entire saw should be around 26 inches in length for an adult of average height. It should be made of fine-tempered steel and have a well-shaped wooden handle that you can grip firmly with your hand. Sight down the blade from the handle to make sure the blade does not bend one way or the other. Even the

*True
Value
Tip*

SMOOTH SAWING

■ After clearly marking a board with the line you intend to cut, position the board so that it will be steady, safe, and easy to cut. This may mean clamping the board to a sturdy surface like a bench or placing it so that you can support the board with your free hand.

■ Begin by sawing back and forth, slowly but firmly, at the top of your line to make a groove.

■ *Let the weight of the saw do most of the downward cutting.*

■ As much as possible, maintain a 60-degree angle (holding the saw two-thirds of the way toward straight up) as you saw.

■ Use the whole blade to saw.

■ Saws rust more easily than other tools, so make sure you keep your handsaw stored vertically in a dry place.

highest quality blade will grow dull over time, which makes it unsafe. As soon as you notice this happening, either sharpen the blade with a saw file (consult your dealer for advice on what to buy and how to use it) or buy a new saw.

MEASUREMENTS AND CONVERSIONS

Measure twice, cut once. Abbreviations and symbols are in parentheses.

LINEAR
U.S.: 12 inches (in/") = 1 foot (ft/'); 3 ft = 1 yard (yd)
metric: 10 millimeters (mm) = 1 centimeter (cm); 100 cm = 1 meter (m)

WEIGHT
U.S.: 16 ounces (oz) = 1 pound (lb)
metric: 1,000 grams (g) = 1 kilogram (kg)

LIQUID VOLUMES
U.S.: 8 ounces or fluid ounces (oz/fl oz) = 1 cup (c); 2 c = 1 pint (pt);
      2 pt = 1 quart (qt); 4 qt = 1 gallon (gal)
metric: 1,000 milliliters (mL) = 1 liter (L)

CONVERTING U.S. AND METRIC

From U.S.	Multiply by	To get metric	From metric	Multiply by	to get U.S.
in	25.4	mm	mm	.0394	in
in	2.54	cm	cm	.3937	in
ft	.3048	m	m	3.2808	ft
yd	.9144	m	m	1.0936	yd
oz	28.350	g	g	.0353	oz
lb	.4536	kg	kg	2.2046	lb
oz/fl oz	29.574	mL	mL	.0338	oz/fl oz
c	.2366	L	L	4.2268	c
pt	.4732	L	L	2.1134	pt
qt	.9464	L	L	1.0567	qt
gal	3.7854	L	L	.2642	gal

■ To cut metal, get a **hacksaw**, which has replaceable blades with much harder teeth than a handsaw. Hacksaws come in a variety of models that are adjustable (usually by wing-nut) to accommodate blades of different sizes. The model you buy should have a fine-tempered, tubular steel frame and a cast-metal, pistol-grip handle that fits comfortably in your hand. A nice feature is a frame that also stores the blades. The model should also take the length(s) of blade you prefer. Hacksaw blades range from 8 to 16 inches long. Different people prefer different blade lengths, according to their individual sawing styles, but popular sizes are 10 and 12 inches. Blades also come in different numbers of teeth per inch (tpi) from a low of 14 (for very thin, soft metal) to a high of 32 (for very thick, hard metal). For starters, buy one blade in the low range, a couple in the mid range, and one in the high range. Be sure to replace a blade as soon as it gets dull or shows wear.

LUMBER SIZES

A 2 × 4 isn't really 2 × 4—it's 1½ × 3¼ inches. Here are the common sizes of lumber in inches.

Listed/Stated	Actual	Listed/Stated	Actual
1 × 2	¾ × 1½	2 × 2	1½ × 1½
1 × 3	¾ × 2½	2 × 3	1½ × 2½
1 × 4	¾ × 3½	2 × 4	1½ × 3¼
1 × 5	¾ × 4¼	2 × 6	1½ × 5½
1 × 6	¾ × 5½	2 × 8	1½ × 7½
1 × 8	¾ × 7¼	2 × 10	1½ × 9¼
1 × 10	¾ × 11¼	2 × 12	1½ × 11¼

KNIVES, CUTTERS, AND SCRAPERS

■ Everyone should have a **pocket knife** for simple cutting, shaving, and slicing tasks. Choose the one that feels the best in your hand. A simple model with one to three blades is fine. Make sure that the blades are made of tempered steel, operate smoothly, and stay securely in place when in use.

■ Get a **putty knife** with a 1-inch blade and a **wall scraper** (sometimes called a wide or large putty knife) with a 4-inch blade. Each is an applicator, spreader, or remover of putty, plaster, or spackle. The highest quality models have one piece of carbon steel for the handle and the blade, a hardwood facing on either side of the handle, and a metal-reinforced handle tip. Test the flexibility of the blade before buying. It should be stiff and springy.

■ Another tool you'll use often is a **utility knife**, with a retractable blade mechanism, for making sharp cuts. Choose any model that features single-edge blades, isn't too light (has some heft), and stores extra blades (reached by removing a central screw). Check to make sure the retraction mechanism works smoothly. Also buy a package of single-edged replacement blades and be sure to change the blade as soon as you notice dullness or wear.

■ Although you may be able to cut most wires with the straight-edge portion of pliers jaws, a better tool for the job—especially for working in cramped spaces or for cutting thin metal—is a **wire cutter**. Get the type called diagonal cutting pliers. The cutting edge is along one side of the tool, allowing you to cut flush against a surface. Look for a model with rubber- or plastic-covered grips.

CHISELING, FILING, SANDING, AND SHARPENING TOOLS

■ A **metal file** sharpens mower blades, garden tool blades or prongs, and the edges of freshly cut metal pipes, sheets, and rods. The best all-purpose model is a 9- to 11-inch, half-round file with both flat and curved surfaces. To clean your metal file, use an inexpensive **file brush** or a wire brush (*see* below).

■ An **oilstone** sharpens hand tool blades. Choose a size that fits well in your hand.

■ Buy several sheets of **sandpaper** in assorted fine and coarse grits. Get a rubber **sanding block** to hold the sandpaper. The most effective kind of block has both flat and rounded surfaces and two slits with metal teeth to hold the paper (which you cut to size).

■ For smoothing rough metal surfaces or fine-polishing wooden ones, buy several grades of **steel wool**.

■ If you anticipate frequent or extensive sanding, or if you simply want to sand much more easily and effectively, consider buying an electric, dual-action **orbital sander**. Consult a dealer to determine which kind of sander best suits your purposes. Different models specialize in (but are not always limited to) different functions: removing big irregularities or old finishes, preparing a clean wooden surface for an applied finish, or the finishing itself.

■ A **wire brush** removes paint, rust, corrosion, or other hard deposits from virtually any surface and cleans away fine debris from files or rasps. Buy any model that feels good in your hand. A nice feature on some models is a scraper built into the handle.

True Value Tip

THE MAGIC OF WD-40

Make sure there's a can of WD-40 in your workshop. It will unstick and unsqueak things all over the house. Its penetrating and dissolving properties also make it an excellent cleaning product that doesn't damage surfaces. Pismo Bob Pringle, owner of the True Value hardware and nursery in Pismo Beach, California, sells WD-40 as a scuff remover, bumper-sticker peeler, and general cleaner.

SHARP IDEAS

True Value Tip

■ Steve Jennings, a True Value customer, knows his saw teeth, shear blades, pick points, and knife or chisel edges are dull when they start reflecting light. When they're sharp, they aren't *thick* enough to be reflecting. He sharpens small scissors and shear blades by cutting with them several times through a folded piece of rough sandpaper (grit-side out). Larger blades, saw teeth, and edges have to be filed or polished with an oilstone.

■ Rubbing chalk on a clean metal file or wood rasp will cut down on clogging.

■ To keep sandpaper from ripping apart, back it with a sheet of adhesive contact paper before you cut it up.

- A **wood chisel** slices away irregular bumps and carves out depressions in wood. Look for a 9½- to 10½-inch carpenter's chisel (also called a pocket chisel) with a wooden handle and a ½- to 1-inch-wide blade that has both a flat edge and a beveled one. The chisel should feel well-balanced in the hand, which means that the handle shouldn't be too light relative to the blade. Most wood chisels should never be pounded with anything heavier than a wooden mallet. If you want a chisel you can hammer, look for one that is metal-capped (you may have to settle for another model that's similar to, but slightly bigger than, a carpenter's chisel).

- A **wood rasp** is for filing down wood surfaces. The best model to get is 9 to 11 inches long with a rectangular profile and coarse teeth. By first using a wood rasp and then sanding, you can perform most repair and maintenance tasks that might otherwise require a plane. Planes are expensive and not often required unless you regularly do carpentry tasks, in which case you need two planes to cover all bases: a **jack plane** for planing with the grain and a **block plane** for planing against the grain.

True Value Tip

CUSTOM BONDS

- Mix a little dust from sanding or sawing into wood glue before applying it. When the mixture dries, it will have the same color as the wood.
- To make an adhesive bond even tighter, follow the advice Scott Haney got from his True Value dealer. After applying glue or cement to one of the two surfaces you want to connect, drop a few strands of steel wool into it. When you clamp the two surfaces together, the steel wool will help hold them in place and, when the adhesive is dry, make the joint even more secure.

GLUES, TAPES, AND FILLERS

■ **Duct tape** is famous for its endless uses. It tightly (and, in most cases, temporarily) binds almost any two surfaces together. You can also use it to cover holes and cracks in pipes and on flat surfaces. It now comes in lots of colors in addition to the signature gray. People use duct tapes in all kinds of ingenious ways. One hardware store owner even spotted a booth at a craft fair selling wallets made entirely of duct tape!

■ **Electrical tape** is used for electrical and plumbing repairs. It's also good for small taping jobs in which waterproofing, camouflage, or ease of removal is a concern.

■ **Epoxy glue**, also called epoxy resin, comes in two tubes and is mixed together right before using. It is good for strongly bonding wood (including joints), materials that are different from each other (such as glass and wood), and plastic.

■ **Hot melt**, which comes in a stick, is extruded by an **electric glue gun**. It sets quickly and holds strongly.

■ **White glue**, also called polyvinyl or PVA glue, is good for light bonding of paper, plastic, ceramic, and wooden joints that will not be under stress.

■ **Wood glue** is a strong glue that's good for indoor woodworking projects. It bonds two pieces of wood and can also fill small holes and cracks.

True Value Tip

OH, NUTS!

When using pliers to turn nuts that are especially tight or that you're concerned about damaging, first wrap the nut or the teeth of the pliers with adhesive tape.

■ **Spackling compound** is ready-mixed plaster that's good for quickly filling in small holes and cracks in plaster or wallboard.

■ **Wood putty** is for filling small holes and gaps in wood. The premixed kind, sold in a small can, is easiest to apply. It tends to dry out, though, while the powdered form can be stored a long time and mixed as needed.

True Value Tip

STEPLADDER TOOL HOLDERS

True Value customer Nick Artega hated it when tools would roll off the stepladder. He drilled several holes in the top steps of his stepladder. Now he has handy holders for screwdrivers, pliers, and other small tools.

LADDERS

■ Choose a **stepladder** that will allow you to comfortably reach your ceilings and upper walls (when painting, cleaning fixtures, changing bulbs, etc.). Depending on your height and that of others in your family and the height of your ceilings, the stepladder you want could be anywhere from 4 to 16 feet high. Choose a stepladder with a hinged framework. If it's more than 5 feet high, it should have a sturdy, fold-out shelf to hold tools, paint cans, and other supplies. The safest and most convenient stepladder is made of fiberglass; it's lightweight and won't conduct electricity, as a metal ladder or sometimes even a wet wooden ladder will. All ladders, including stepladders, are manufactured according to strict safety guidelines and are given a rating that reflects their loading capacity (the weight they will bear): light-duty (200 pounds), medium-duty (225 pounds), heavy-duty (250 pounds), and extra-heavy-duty (300 pounds). Choose a ladder that will support the heaviest person who will be using it plus at least a 10-pound margin.

■ For cleaning gutters, checking out roof problems, and painting the outside of the house, you'll need an **extension ladder**. Look for an aluminum one with flat rungs. A type 2 or commercial ladder is recommended for its safety and durability.

True Value Tip

TALL LADDER SAFETY

■ Always carry a ladder upright, not slanted. Support one vertical rail against your chest and thigh. Grip one rung at thigh height and the other at head height.

■ Set the base of the ladder about 2 feet from the wall and slowly lean the top against the wall.

■ If you're using an extension ladder, extend the upper part 6 inches beyond where you want the top to rest. The top portion of the ladder should always overlap the bottom portion by at least one-quarter of the top portion's length.

■ Finally, move the bottom of the ladder away from the wall to a distance that's at least a quarter the length of the ladder. This arrangement will help keep the ladder firmly in place as you work on it.

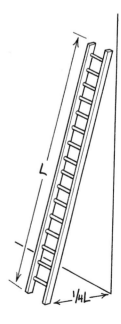

TOOLBOXES

There are **toolboxes** of many sizes, materials, features, and configurations. The right one depends on what you like and what your needs are. For example, you may have the space and the desire to store your tools and supplies on racks, pegboards, or shelves, or inside cabinet drawers. If so, you may want a small toolbox—perhaps just a tool tray—that you can use to organize and transport the tools for a specific job. If you have strong muscles and limited storage space, you may prefer to keep all your basic tools and supplies in one box, in which case it needs to be especially durable and have compartments of various sizes. Most people find it handy to have at least one main toolbox that can store most of their everyday tools—except for the larger ones, like saws—and a certain amount of their most frequently used and least bulky supplies, like tubes of glue, some nails and screws, a roll of wire, a few sheets of sandpaper, and so on. Here are some general guidelines for choosing a toolbox:

■ Boxes made of hard, rubberized or plastic material withstand a lot of physical abuse, are lighter and more water-resistant than wooden or metal boxes, and protect tools from damage during storage.

■ The box should have one or two hard handles, mounted on rotating pins, across the length of the box that can be easily raised and lowered.

■ The lid of the box should have a secure latch that can be easily opened and closed and, if appropriate, has a child-proof lock.

■ A good feature is a lift-out tray with its own handle that can be used to assemble a limited number of tools and supplies for a specific job.

■ If the box is bigger than 12 inches high by 10 inches wide by 20 inches long, it should be divided into at least two or three compartments so tools won't bang into one another when the box is carried, dropped, or upset. Investigate tool organizers that go inside boxes to keep tools in place.

True Value Tip

RUST BUSTERS
■ To keep infrequently used tools and supplies from rusting inside your toolbox or drawer, True Value dealer Eugene Duff in Beaverton, Oregon, suggests fitting a piece of old carpet into the bottom and giving it an occasional shot of WD-40 or light machine oil.
■ Troy Landerson, a True Value customer who lives in an often sultry city, keeps a charcoal briquette inside his toolbox to absorb moisture.
■ To remove rust from nuts, bolts, or screws, soak them for a couple hours in a container of cola soft drink. In a couple of hours, the rust will be gone.

CLEANING TOOLS AND SUPPLIES
Another category of tools are those used for cleaning your home. Here again, good tools and supplies will make the jobs easier and faster. Here are the essential cleaning tools for doing battle with all kinds of dirt:

■ A **corn straw broom** is more durable than a synthetic broom. The natural material stays cleaner because its tips release dirt and dust better than the split ends of synthetic fibers. Pick a

INVISIBLE FORCE FIELDS

While you're assembling your basic cleaning products, add a surface protector. These products make it much easier to clean your counters, appliances, tile, stainless-steel sink, and other shiny surfaces. A surface protector will repel water, soil, stains, soap scum, and mineral deposits, prevent buildup, and speed up your cleaning time.

broom with bristles that are even across the bottom. A small **whisk broom** (again, preferably corn straw) is handy for cleaning steps, corners, and small messes. For your sidewalks, driveway, and garage, get an 18-inch **push broom** with coarse bristles. Buy a **dustpan** that can collect all these sweepings. A long-handled model saves bending. Choose one with a sturdy, commercial-grade handle, not a wire one.

■ A good multipurpose **scrubbing brush** is a 6-inch model with nylon bristles. A natural fiber (palmyra) brush costs less but is not as durable. Pick a brush with a handle that raises your hand off the surface so that you don't smash your knuckles while you're scrubbing. A special brush well worth having is a **grout and tile brush**. Its stiff bristles clean corners and spaces between tiles much better than, for example, an old toothbrush. You will also need a special brush for cleaning the toilet; a covered holder makes storage of this brush more convenient.

■ You'll need **cloths** for cleaning and polishing. Cotton is the most absorbent fiber. You can buy cleaning cloths or make them from old diapers, T-shirts, flannel shirts, or towels. Keep a stack, since you'll switch to a fresh cloth several times while doing a major cleaning job.

■ A **duster** is a mass of natural lamb's wool or synthetic fibers fastened to a stick. The lanolin in wool makes an especially good dust magnet. Choose a duster with a long or telescoping handle so you can extend your reach to high surfaces and cobwebs.

■ To wash floors, the best choice is a **sponge mop**. Cotton ones are good for swabbing but not scrubbing, and they're difficult to clean. Choose a sponge mop that enables you to change the sponge easily. You may also want a mop that combines a sponge head with a scrubbing surface. Make sure the handle is long enough that you don't need to stoop while cleaning. A squeezing mechanism in the middle of the handle, rather than on the sponge, reduces bending and accidental messes. If you have wood floors, also get a dry **dust mop** or, better yet, a canister vacuum (see below).

■ Buy an **upright vacuum** with a powerful beater brush to clean dirt from rugs and carpets. A **canister vacuum** is best for other floor surfaces; look for a model with a crevice tool, an upholstery brush, and an extender rod for reaching overhead. If you can buy only one vacuum, a canister that incorporates a beater brush can do both jobs, but less easily. Portable, handheld vacuums are convenient for quick clean-up of spills but not powerful enough to be your only vacuum. A wet/dry vacuum is useful for big messes and liquid spills. For all vacuums, always keep **spare bags** on hand.

■ A **scraper**, such as a plastic paint scraper, is great to remove baked-on spills from ovens and stoves and bits of goo from wooden, tile, or vinyl floors.

■ Get a variety of **large and small synthetic sponges** (stronger than natural sponges) for all-purpose cleaning and some **combination sponge-and-scrub pads** (gentler than steel wool) for tough dirt and stains.

■ For cleaning windows, you'll need a good **squeegee** with a metal handle and a rubber edge (and, if desired, a telescoping handle to reach upstairs windows from outside).

■ The following **cleaning supplies in bottles and boxes** will handle practically anything that comes your way (keep mixtures in sturdy spray bottles ready to use): an all-purpose spray cleaner, a tile cleaner for removing mildew and soap scum (preferably with a high concentration of bleach), baking soda, ammonia (clear, not scented or sudsing), liquid chlorine bleach, and scouring powder.

True Value Tip

SAFETY WITH CLEANING SUPPLIES
■ Read all manufacturer's warnings on the labels of all cleaning supplies.
■ Store all cleaning supplies safely out of reach of young children.
■ Never mix ammonia, or supplies containing ammonia, with bleach because the combination releases deadly fumes.
■ Use bleach in well-ventilated areas, and try not to inhale the fumes. Wear rubber gloves to protect your hands. Bleach will permanently remove color from clothing and can weaken gold rings.
■ To find out if scouring powder will scratch a particular surface, first test the product on a small, inconspicuous area.

THE MIGHTY LITTLE BOX

True Value Tip

Baking soda can be used in a multitude of ways around the house. Because it contains no bleach or phosphates, it's safer for the environment and causes fewer allergic reactions than chemical products. Baking soda can clean and freshen your:

■ **Refrigerator:** Place an open box of baking soda, with the date marked in big numbers on the box, inside the refrigerator to absorb odors. Replace it every 2 months.

■ **Microwave:** Mix 2 tablespoons of baking soda with 1 cup of water. Place it in the microwave and run on high for 3 minutes. Wipe the inside of the microwave with a damp sponge.

■ **Nonstick pans:** Mix 1 cup of water, ½ cup of white vinegar, and 2 tablespoons of baking soda in the pan and boil for 10 minutes.

■ **Food burnt or baked onto a stove, oven, casserole dish, or nonstick pan:** Cover with baking soda. Pour on enough boiling water to make a thick paste, and let soak for 15 minutes. Rinse with clear water.

■ **Drains:** Pour ½ cup of baking soda and 1 cup of white vinegar into the drain. Let it foam up, then flush with hot water followed by cold water.

■ **Sink and tub:** Scrub with baking soda moistened with a little water.

■ **Toilet bowl:** Pour 1½ cups of white vinegar into the toilet bowl and add ½ cup of baking soda. Let it stand for an hour or so.

■ **Carpet:** To remove odors, sprinkle baking soda on the carpet and let it stand, then vacuum.

■ **Smelly containers:** Sprinkle baking soda into diaper pails, garbage cans, and pet litter boxes to absorb odors.

■ **Laundry:** To keep dirty clothes from getting smelly between laundry days, sprinkle baking soda between the layers in a hamper or basket. Add ½ cup to your washer along with the detergent to give the laundry extra freshness.

■ **Grease and oil stains:** Cover a spot on a garage floor or cement driveway with a layer of baking soda mixed with mason's sand, or just use plain baking soda. Let it stand overnight, then sweep. If any stains remain, scrub them with baking soda and a stiff brush.

YOUR WORKSHOP

■ Tape or nail a yardstick to one edge of your workbench. You'll be surprised how often it comes in handy to measure things quickly and easily.

■ Mike Devlin, True Value dealer in Albany, New York, recommends fastening a block of plastic foam to your workbench or a nearby storage shelf. You can use it to hold all sorts of small items, like drill bits, screws, nails, knives, screwdrivers, and parts—either temporarily, while you're working on a particular job, or over the long term.

■ True Value customer Tracy LaSalle keeps a supply of inexpensive craft sticks ("Popsicle sticks") in her workshop. She constantly finds new uses for them: mixing epoxy, smoothing putty seams, padding vise and clamp jaws, etc.

■ Pat Torrero turned a large closet into a small but perfectly adequate workshop. She put up storage shelves on one wall and a pegboard for holding tools on another. To create a sturdy work surface just inside the closet door, she covered the top of a beat-up workbench with a sheet of ¼-inch plywood and then nailed tempered hardboard onto the plywood. When the hardboard gets worn, she can pull out the nails, flip it over, and have a brand new top. A scrap piece of carpet on one side of the bench serves as a protective, temporary resting spot for tools. She painted everything in her workshop white—walls, floors, shelves, pegboard, and bench—so that small items show up better, and she used a semigloss finish for easy cleaning and no glare.

■ John Fix, True Value dealer in Eastchester, New York, recommends keeping one or two empty shoe boxes near your workbench or toolbox. They make excellent temporary carriers for a project. Carry just the tools you need, plus all the nuts, bolts, and parts you remove or want to use.

■ Durable plastic food containers, which come in a variety of sizes and configurations, make excellent storage containers inside your toolbox, not only for small items like nails, drill bits, and glue tubes but for hard, flat tools like wrenches, files, putty knives, and utility knifes.

❷ Handyperson of the Year

A 12-Month Planner

When you have a house, there's always something to do. In fact, it's easy to forget an important maintenance job because you're busy with other things. This basic calendar of tasks will help you stay organized and efficient in taking care of your home. Think of it as a master "to do list." It will enable you to keep a regular maintenance routine so you can catch problems when they're still little and easily fixed. It will also help you spread out the big jobs so you won't find yourself swamped, particularly during months when seasons are changing. Finally, it will guide you to take on projects at the best times of the year for doing them.

Play with the calendar as you move through the year. Modify the timing of outdoor chores, including gardening, to reflect your local climate. Add items that suit your situation. Keep your own monthly and yearly records in a special notebook or calendar, stating what you've done, what you need to do at a later date, and what you could do *anytime* you have an hour or two to spare.

JANUARY

■ In the spirit of New Year resolutions, tidy up and review all household maintenance records to remind yourself of the tasks that need to be done, or would be nice to do, during the coming year. If you haven't been keeping a household maintenance notebook, start one now.

■ If you have a forced-air furnace, clean or replace the filter.

■ Get nursery and garden store catalogs and begin dreaming about the spring planting season.

■ In cold climates, this is the best time of year to cut firewood. The wood is easiest to cut, it'll season over the summer and be ready by next fall, and you'll get some hearty exercise. It's said that in winter, wood warms you twice!

■ Remove heavy snow from tree branches, shrubs, porches, decks, and even roofs as soon as possible.

FEBRUARY

■ Check the lower edges of your roof for ice dams and if necessary repair (*see* Chapter 9).

■ Check indoor spaces below these spots on the roof to make sure you have adequate, undamaged insulation and ventilation. If you don't or if you can't tell, consult a hardware store or home care professional.

■ Get a jump on spring planting. To determine how best to fertilize gardens, shrubs, or trees, take a soil sample from each relevant location, put it in a separate, well-labeled plastic bag, and send all samples for a free analysis to your local United States Department of Agriculture (USDA) Cooperative Extension Service (usually listed in the government pages of the phone book). Submitting samples in February, when demand is relatively light, will guarantee the fastest and most timely service.

■ Do the monthly cleaning or replacing of your furnace filter.

■ Take advantage of being confined indoors to do simple interior repair and maintenance tasks that don't require much ventilation or cover much space.

MARCH

■ Drain your hot-water heater to remove deposits (*see* Chapter 6). It's easy to do and, over the years, makes a significant difference in how well your heater performs and how long it lasts.

■ Inspect roof shingles for damage and repair or replace individual shingles as necessary. Also, check metal flashings around rooftop chimneys, vents, dormers, eaves, and roof edges to ensure that they're watertight against spring rains (*see* Chapter 9).

■ Make sure your lawn mover and garden tools are in good shape. Clean away any dirt or rust. Sharpen blades and cutting surfaces. Repair or replace cracked handles and loose parts.

■ If the snow has melted and the ground thawed, rake leaves and remove debris from your lawn. Don't bear down too hard on tender young grass.

■ Saw or remove broken branches from trees, shrubs, and bushes before new growth starts. Check a local nursery for advice on pruning specific trees and plantings.

■ In warmer areas, plant ground covers and turn garden soil. Otherwise, these tasks can wait until April or early May.

■ Do the monthly cleaning or replacing of your furnace filter.

APRIL

■ Scrutinize all windows and their frames. Repair or replace damaged moldings and panes, take down storm windows, and inspect, repair, and install screens (*see* Chapter 5).

■ Clean the gutters. Then, on a day when it's raining heavily and steadily, put on your rain gear and inspect all the gutters and down spouts for signs of leaks, clogs, and sagging or broken supports. Note whether the down spouts are carrying water far enough away from the house. Mark, sketch, or note all trouble spots and make repairs as soon as possible after the deluge (*see* Chapter 9).

■ Time for termite patrol (*see* Chapter 9).

■ After the danger of hard frost is past, turn the outdoor faucets back on. Open and close outdoor faucets to make sure they work properly. Fill hoses to find out if they leak and need repair or replacement. Inspect sprinklers and, with soapy water and a wire brush, clean away any rust or deposits blocking their holes.

■ If the danger of hard frost or heavy snowfall has passed, begin digging in the garden and planting (*see* Chapter 10).

MAY

■ Inspect masonry on or around the house and property for any damage over the winter months. Repair cracks and, where necessary, enhance protection from moisture (*see* Chapter 9).

■ Attention would-be gardeners in cold-weather climates: If you haven't already begun serious work (breaking and turning the soil, fertilizing, planting, transplanting), this month is your last opportunity to take full advantage of the growing season.

■ Do exterior painting, staining, or water sealing tasks before hot weather comes. This relatively cooler month allows slower drying time and, therefore, better surface bonding and durability. Also, if you're doing these tasks yourself, you'll be more comfortable now than you would be in the heat of midsummer.

■ Clean and if necessary repair constructed ponds, fountains, and swimming pools, so they'll be in sparkling condition for summer.

■ Inspect and if necessary service air conditioners and fans to make sure they function properly.

JUNE

■ Using a flashlight, carefully inspect the inside of the chimney (with damper wide open) for creosote deposits. These deposits can cause not only inefficient and extremely hazardous burning but unpleasant smells in hot, humid weather. If the chimney is dirty—and it definitely is if more than half of the interior surface is coated with lumpy black creosote—call a sweep. Also, check fireplace ventilators and ash traps and clean them if necessary. Then close the damper tightly and keep it closed throughout the warm weather.

■ Watch for signs of unwanted insects in the garden (for example, chew holes in leaves) and around the home (for example, swarming or nests near the house) so you can stop any damage before it gets worse (*see* Chapter 9).

■ Look out for holes and mounds in your property that may indicate a rodent invasion. You may even sight the culprits themselves: moles, voles, chipmunks, or groundhogs booby-trapping your lawn and breakfasting on your flower buds or lettuce leaves. Consult a professional for advice on discouraging or safely getting rid of these invaders. Many areas have laws against taking matters in your own hands, plus you don't want to use traps or poisons that may jeopardize humans, other animals, your plantings, or groundwater.

■ If you have a septic tank, now is the most settled time to check it out: after the spring rains are over and before the more dramatic weather of summer stirs things up (*see* Chapter 6). If the tank is more than half full of sludge, have it emptied by a professional.

■ Clean the inside of all toilet tanks, where mineral deposits can eventually cause major problems. If necessary, insulate the inside and/or the outside to prevent sweating in the hot weather to come (*see* Chapter 6).

■ Air out bedding, camping gear, and musty furniture in a sunny, outdoor place—preferably on a porch, deck, sidewalk, or driveway rather than on the grass (which is in its high-growth season).

■ If you intend to order firewood for the winter, do it now. Most suppliers charge lower rates during the summer months, and you'll be assured that the wood will have at least three months of seasoning before burning. Also, if you're stacking it yourself, you'll probably be more comfortable doing it now than in the hotter months.

JULY

■ Give all air-conditioning units their first monthly cleaning of the summer (*see* Chapter 8).

■ Inspect the kitchen exhaust fan. Clean grease deposits from the filter and, if necessary, the motor and fan assembly (more easily done when the hot weather outdoors helps melt the grease).

■ For the health of your house, it's time to get down and dirty. Look for wood rot or decay in crawl spaces alongside and underneath the house. Where it's present, you need to improve ventilation and/or add a moisture barrier (*see* Chapter 3).

■ This is a good time to paint radiators, registers, and heating-system baseboards. You want to do this when the heat is off so the paint has time to cure.

AUGUST

■ Once again, give air-conditioning units their monthly cleaning (*see* July).

■ Perform any major patching or sealing tasks on the roof, gutters, or paved driveways and sidewalks. Yes, hot weather can cause unpleasant working conditions, but cements, glues, and sealers apply much more easily and bond much more securely in the heat, so it's well worth the sweat (*see* Chapter 9).

■ Have your indoor heating system inspected, and do any necessary repairs so it will be ready to function well by the time cold weather comes (*see* Chapter 8). If you use furnace filters, stock up now for the winter.

SEPTEMBER

■ Do any remaining exterior painting, staining, or water sealing tasks that you want to get done before the winter. Plan to finish these tasks before any leaves begin to fall.

■ Do any pre-winter pruning, dividing, or transplanting now, well in advance of the first frost.

■ Make sure you're fully stocked with winter firewood.

■ Install any additional home insulation that is needed.

■ If you live in an area of the country where the winters are cold, review all the October tasks below. In cold-winter climates, October is the busiest time of the year for home maintenance and repair tasks. Anything you can do in September will help lighten the load.

OCTOBER

■ Time to put your garden to bed for the winter. As soon as it has ceased producing, cut down all stalks (otherwise they can lead freezing water into the ground), turn the soil, and cover it with a thin layer of mulch, leaves, grass, or straw. If the mulch is relatively light and exposed, secure it with overlying sheets of chicken-wire or other screening held down by strategically placed bricks or rocks.

■ When the weather starts to cool, remove window screens and install storm windows. Then inspect all doors (interior and exterior) and windows to make sure they open and close properly, without sticking, moving too freely, or leaving big gaps. If necessary, repair or replace them (*see* Chapter 5).

■ Check the caulking, weather stripping, and gaps around doors and exterior windows. Do any necessary repairs (*see* Chapter 5).

■ Clean air-conditioning units. If practical, remove and store them for the winter. If not, wrap the outside of each unit securely with weather-resistant canvas or a similar protective covering.

■ Clean and repair outdoor furniture and tools, including the lawn mower, before storing them for the winter. If certain items need replacing, now is the best time to do so: Prices are lower, thanks to end-of-the-season sales, and you'll be sure of having the item ready at hand when the weather turns.

■ Make sure all snow removal equipment is in good condition and easily accessible.

■ Drain, clean, and, if necessary, cover outdoor pools, fountains, and ponds.

■ Plant bulbs that you want to bloom in the spring: for example, daffodils, tulips, or crocuses. They should be in the ground for a few weeks before the first hard frost.

■ If you reside in a cold-weather climate and intend to have a live Christmas tree that you'll later replant in your yard, dig the hole for it now, before the ground freezes. Fill the hole with leaves, grass clippings, straw, or gravel until after Christmas, when you'll be planting the tree, and save the dirt for the planting in a bag or container stored where it won't freeze. If you want to get your tree from a nursery, order it now to make sure it's available.

■ Begin raking leaves from the lawn when most of them have fallen from the trees. If you have a mulching mower, consider mowing over some of the leaves instead of raking them to create a thin layer of mulch for the lawn over the winter.

■ Do the monthly cleaning or replacing of your furnace filter.

NOVEMBER

■ Finish raking leaves from the lawn before the first hard frost.

■ Re-seed thin or bare spots in the grass now. Many, if not most, of the seeds will lie dormant over the winter months and activate themselves as soon as conditions are favorable in the spring (*see* Chapter 10).

■ In harsh-winter climates, place mulch (or leaf piles) around outdoor trees, shrubs, and plants before the first hard frost.

■ Drain and store all hoses. Shut off all outdoor faucets.

■ Make sure all outside pipes—or pipes in non-insulated areas—are drained or protected from freezing. If not, wrap them tightly in insulation held in place by duct tape (consult your hardware store dealer for proper R-value and wrapping instructions).

■ After all the leaves have fallen, clean your roof gutters and down spouts of debris (*see* Chapter 9).

■ Do the monthly cleaning or replacing of your furnace filter.

DECEMBER

■ Make sure your home is adequately equipped to cope with power failures, especially in cold climates or in hurricane areas. Stock up on candles, flashlights, nonperishable food items, and non-electric heaters.

■ Check to see that all outlets, receptacles, cords, and plugs are in good condition. If not, make necessary repairs and replacements (*see* Chapter 7).

■ Stock up on materials like sand or kitty litter that will help melt ice and/or provide traction on outdoor steps, walkways, and driveways.

■ Now and throughout the winter, remove heavy snow from tree branches, shrubs, porches, decks, and even roofs as soon as possible.

■ Do the monthly cleaning or replacing of your furnace filter.

■ Pat yourself on the back for 12 months of good house tending and mending!

③ The Inside Story
Floors, Ceilings, and Walls

Often you don't notice them until you've settled back for a few moments of peace: the squeaky floorboards, the tiny cracks in the wall, the gray spots on the ceiling. They may be minor irritations for a while, easily ignored, but if you neglect them for too long, they may turn into catastrophes. And bear in mind that the state of your floors, ceilings, and walls affects the well-being of the support systems beneath, below, and behind them: your home's electricity, plumbing, heating, cooling—even the structure of the building itself. So get out of your easy chair and get to work!

Emergency

SAGGING OR LEAKING CEILING

A leaking or sagging ceiling can indicate a serious structural problem, significant plumbing damage, or at the very least a major mess in the making, so you'll want to address the situation right away.

■ If you see a crack or a brown or gray spot on the ceiling, don't wait for a drip to appear before you take action. Drill a small hole in the center of the crack or spot and put a bucket directly below it to catch leaking water. It may not be pretty, but the alternative could be your ceiling suddenly crashing down on you!

■ If the ceiling is wet or leaking, first put a large bucket under the spot to catch any drips. Then remove everything else below it and cover the floor to catch any falling ceiling pieces and slow down any flow of water. Best is plastic sheeting, but an old cloth sheet is better than nothing. After you cover up, look for possible sources of the leak. Do this even if the ceiling is sagging but not actually showing moisture, since water can collect behind plaster or particleboard long before it soaks through.

■ If the ceiling is leaking or you suspect a leak, try tracing the leak to the roof. Inspect any room, attic, eave, or crawl space between the ceiling and the roof for signs of leakage, and if you find a leak, stop it at its source (*see* Leaky Roof, in Chapter 9).

■ If you can't find any signs of leaking above the ceiling, try to determine if a nearby pipe is the source. To do this, you will need some sense of how your plumbing system is laid out. Remember that water travels easily, so the spot where the *ceiling* is leaking may be somewhat removed from the spot where the *pipe* is leaking. After an initial review, turn off the water supply and observe whether the leak eventually slows or even stops. If it does, you have good evidence that the source is a leaky pipe. For a temporary patch, see the beginning of Chapter 6, then call a plumber.

■ A sagging ceiling can also be caused by a structural defect in the building. If you think that's the problem, talk to a contractor about correcting the defect, then repairing or replacing the ceiling.

Know-how

PERFECT PLASTER PATCHING

A sloppy patch is almost as ugly as the original crack or hole. With these simple tricks, you can pull off an almost invisible repair.

Small cracks or holes

1. Clear away any loose plaster surrounding the crack or hole.

2. Using a small, sharp-edged knife, carefully scrape plaster from the inside edge of the crack or hole so that it's slightly wider on the bottom than the top.

3. Dampen the area inside the crack or hole with a wet paintbrush, then apply new plaster or spackling compound (the latter is easier and just as effective) with a putty knife. Press the mixture down to make sure that it fills the crack or hole, then smooth it flush with the wall. Err on the side of overfilling rather than underfilling because you'll be sanding the patch later.

4. When the patch is completely dry, sand it smooth with fine sandpaper. Then prime and repaint it or patch it with wallpaper.

Large cracks or holes

Follow essentially the same process, but don't try to fill in the crack or hole all at once with new plaster or spackling compound. A large amount of wet mixture won't stay in place or form a strong bond while drying.

■ If the crack or hole is less than 2 inches wide, apply a thin layer of mixture across the bottom. Let it dry before applying and smoothing the final layer on top of it. When that layer has dried, sand the patch smooth.

■ If the crack or hole is more than 2 inches across, begin by applying a ring of mixture 1 inch wide around the inside edges of the crack or hole. Smooth out the top of this ring and let it dry. Then apply a smaller ring inside this one, smooth it out, and let it dry. Continue this pattern until you close up the crack or hole. After the patch has dried, sand it smooth.

■ If the hole is deep, you may have to fill it up to patching level with wadded newspaper (ideally topped by a piece of screening) before applying the first thin layer of plaster or spackling compound. An alternative is to use a drywall patch (*see* A Hole in the Wall below).

A HOLE IN THE WALL

Drywall looks much stronger than it really is. One false bang, bump, or slip and a hole suddenly appears. If the hole is small and not too deep, you can patch it with plaster or spackling compound (see above). Otherwise, here's how to apply a drywall patch:

1. From a scrap piece of drywall (preferably the same kind as the original wall), cut out a square patch slightly larger than the hole plus any surrounding area that's cracked or damaged. Lay the patch over the hole, covering all the damage, and trace around it.

2. Using a drywall saw (ideal for the job, it looks like a knife with a jagged edge) or a knife with a longish "poke" blade, cut out the square in the wall.

3. Find or create a wooden board that's at least 1 inch thick, considerably narrower than the square, and at least 4 inches longer than the width of the square.

4. Maneuver the board inside the hole and hold it horizontal with at least 2 inches extending

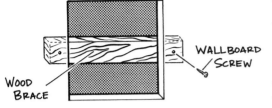

WALLBOARD SCREW

WOOD BRACE

beyond both sides. Hold the board in place until step 5 is completed.

5. Drill starting holes, then insert flat-headed, countersunk screws through the drywall on either side of the square into the board behind. Keep screwing until the heads dig slightly below the surface.

6. Apply plaster or spackling compound to all four edges of the square patch and to the back of the patch where it will come in contact with the board you've just screwed into place. Insert the patch carefully into the square hole and press it against the board. Hold it there for 1 or 2 minutes.

PATCH

JOINT COMPOUND

7. With a putty knife, apply dabs of mixture on the two screw holes. Then scrape away excess mixture on the patch and the screw holes with a putty knife. Smooth the mixture so that it's perfectly flush with the surrounding wallboard surface. If the wall surface is textured, score the mixture with a putty knife or stiff brush so the patch has the same look.

8. After the mixture has completely dried, fill in, smooth, and (if appropriate) texture any remaining cracks and allow them to dry. When the patch is complete, lightly sand any spots that aren't flush with the wall or ceiling. Then prime and repaint it or patch it with wallpaper.

PLASTERING LIKE A PRO

■ When you're plastering over a large, shallow depression in a wall or ceiling, make the bond stronger and more consistent by giving the plaster some inner supports to cling to. Tap staples into the depressed area at random spots, so that the staples protrude slightly, but not above the finished surface level. To do this with a staple gun, tape a thin (about ¹⁄₁₆ inch) strip of wood to the bottom of the gun to keep the staples from being fully inserted. When you apply the plaster, it will attach to, and harden around, the staples.

■ When you're involved in a lengthy plastering or spackling job, you can keep your plaster moist and pliable twice as long by stirring in a small amount of white vinegar: about 2 tablespoons per quart.

■ For smoother, less visible seams between wallboard or drywall panels, rub the compound with a wet towel or sponge immediately after application. This helps create a level, even, tight bond that requires little or no sanding when dry.

■ Occasionally a nail will pop out of a drywall or wallboard wall, often causing a bulge in the wall. If you just hammer the nail back in place, it's bound to pop out again. Here's a more lasting solution: Hammer a new nail into the wall about 1 inch above the popped-out nail, so that the head goes slightly below the surface. This secures the wall. Using a nail set or another nail, drive the popped-out nail into the wall, much deeper in than you drove the other nail. Cover both nail depressions with a patch of spackling compound. Let the compound dry and then sand it and paint.

■ Small, recurring cracks in wall plaster, commonly at corners and around door and window frames, are called stress cracks. They happen when your house settles or adjusts to seasonal differences in humidity and temperature. Instead of repeatedly filling in the cracks, cover them with specially meshed wall tape (available at hardware stores), which you can then paint to match the wall.

■ When you drill into a plaster wall, plaster can spray all over the place. To catch it, tape a small paper bag directly underneath and pull it open to catch debris. Then place a strip of masking tape on the exact spot and start drilling. For plaster ceilings, place a strip of tape on the spot and, holding a plastic coffee-can lid up against it to collect debris, drill through the lid into the ceiling. Whenever you're drilling, don't forget to wear goggles to protect your eyes!

■ Want to get rid of unwanted plaster streaks and clumps on porcelain, metal, brick, or concrete? For hard, nonporous surfaces like porcelain or metal, just soften the plaster with hot water (it might take repeated applications or soaking under a rag) and gently scrub it off with a stiff-bristled brush. For crumbly, porous surfaces like brick or concrete, use a solution of 1 part muriatic acid to 10 parts water. Wearing rubber gloves and being careful not to get the solution on your skin or clothing or any other surface, apply it to the plaster with a stiff-bristled brush. If this fails to do the job, add a bit more muriatic acid to the mixture (up to a 1:4 acid-water ratio).

STOPPING SQUEAKS

When a board squeaks, it's crying out, "Help! Something's rubbing me the wrong way!" A spot in a floor squeaks because two floorboards are rubbing together. A stair squeaks because the tread (horizontal board) is rubbing against its supporting riser (vertical board), the riser mounted on top of it, and/or the stringer along the side (angled board on which all the stairs sit).

An easy way to stop such squeaks, at least for a while, is to lubricate the space between squeaking boards by squeezing graphite powder from a tube between the joints. More permanent repairs call for more heroic measures. Ideally, remove any carpeting or runner on the stairs before working on the wood below.

Squeaky floorboards, if you can get under them

1. Ask someone else to walk on the floor so that you can pinpoint squeaky areas as well as other parts of the floor where boards are loose.

2. If possible, hammer thin wedges of wood between the subflooring (the boards under the floorboards) and the nearest supporting joist on either side of a squeak. You can buy wedges at a hardware store or make your own. Before inserting them, coat each side with a thin layer of wood glue.

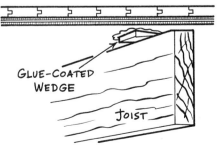

GLUE-COATED
WEDGE

JOIST

3. Insert wood screws through the subflooring into the centers of the two squeaking boards, to attach them more firmly to the subflooring. *Before inserting the screws, make sure they are not so long that they will break through the floorboards.* Insert screws not only where the boards squeak but anywhere else along the two boards—or along other boards—where they're loose.

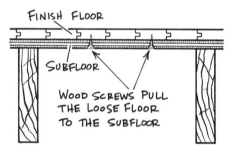

FINISH FLOOR

SUBFLOOR

WOOD SCREWS PULL
THE LOOSE FLOOR
TO THE SUBFLOOR

Squeaky floorboards, if you can't get under them

1. Hammer finishing nails at several points between the two floorboards to keep them from rubbing together. Angle the nails instead of nailing them straight in so they're less likely to work back out. If possible, create an even better bond by hammering finishing nails directly into the edge of one squeaking board at such an angle that they also go through the adjacent squeaking board.

2. If this procedure doesn't stop one or both of the boards from squeaking, the problem lies between one or both of the boards and the subflooring. To secure a board to the subflooring, hammer finishing nails at several points along its center. For each nail, drill a pilot hole first, drive it below the surface with a nail set or another nail (at an angle so it's less likely to work back out), and cover the head with wood filler.

Squeaky stairs, if you can get under the stairway

1. Have someone walk on the stairs so you can pinpoint all squeaking areas.

2. If possible, hammer a thin wedge of wood, coated with wood glue, between each squeaking tread and its supporting riser, the riser in back of it, and the springer on each side. Then, if possible, nail each wedge securely in place, going up through the wedge and being careful to pick the smallest possible nail that will connect the two surfaces.

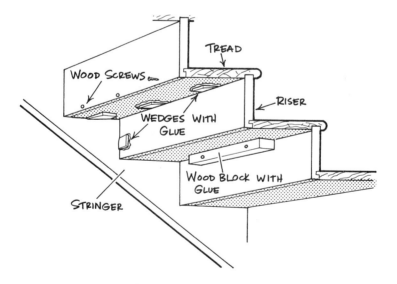

3. If you can't drive in the wedges, secure the area between the tread and its supporting riser with a wooden block. First, cut from a 1-by-2-inch piece of wood a piece at least two-thirds as long as the tread. Coat each inside surface of the block with wood glue. Then nail the block firmly into the corner formed by the tread and the supporting riser, so that the 2-inch side presses against the riser and the 1-inch side against the tread.

Squeaky stairs, if you can't get under the stairway

1. After making pilot holes, drive finishing nails at an angle through the squeaking tread into the supporting riser.

2. Also drive finishing nails through the tread into the stringer on either side.

3. On exposed wood, drive the nail heads below the surface with a nail set or another nail and cover them with wood filler.

REPLACING A CERAMIC TILE

A broken, chipped, or discolored tile is easy to replace. Wear goggles for safety.

1. Remove the grout around all sides of the old tile with a grout saw (available for a reasonable price at hardware stores).

2. Using a glass cutter, score the old tile with two crossed lines, one running from each corner to the opposite corner.

3. Tap the center of the old tile, where the crosslines meet, with a chisel (a "cold chisel," not a woodworking chisel) and a mallet or hammer. Start gently and add a bit more force with each tap until the tile breaks neatly into four pieces.

4. Clean out any old grout that remains in the tile space with a pick, wire brush, or grout saw.

5. Apply adhesive to the back of the replacement tile and ease it into place. Put toothpicks all around it to hold it centered in the space. Hold it there with masking tape until the adhesive has dried.

6. Regrout the tile in place. To match the color of the rest of the grout, you may have to mix it with coloring (available at hardware stores) before grouting.

True Value Tip

VINYL TILES

■ Removing vinyl tile—to replace either a single tile or an entire floor—can be a messy, long, even hazardous job if you use a heat gun or a mallet and chisel. True Value dealers suggest laying a cloth on top of a single tile and ironing over it with slow, firm strokes for a minute or two. It should lift right up. Then move on to the next tile, if you're removing more than one.

■ Adhesive tiles stick best if the adhesive is pliable. Sean Gallagher's True Value dealer gave him this practical advice: To loosen up the adhesive before applying tiles, set them in the sun or in a warm window for at least an hour before removing the backing.

■ To create a nearly invisible cover-up for a small hole, gouge, or tear in vinyl or linoleum flooring, take a piece of scrap that's the same color, shave a thin layer off the top, and chop it into tiny pieces (the size of ice-cream sprinkles). Form a paste by mixing these pieces with clear shellac or varnish and use the paste to fill in the damaged spot. When it's dry, you can't tell the difference.

HANGING IT UP

When you're putting something on a plaster or wallboard wall, you want to make sure it stays put or it could bring part of the wall down with it, not to mention break that picture or mirror. The most secure place to insert a nail or screw is into a wooden stud that forms a vertical support behind the plaster or wallboard. In most wooden wall frames, the studs are 16 inches apart. (*See* Five Ways to Find a Stud below.) If there is no stud behind the place where you want to hang something, use the appropriate fastener to hold the object in place against the plaster or wallboard itself.

True Value Tip

FIVE WAYS TO FIND A STUD

■ Tap the wall with your knuckles in various places, listening closely. Taps on top of a stud will not sound hollow; taps between studs will.

■ Run a magnetized stud finder (available at hardware stores) over the wall. Stop immediately whenever the interior magnet stands rigidly perpendicular to the wall, which indicates that it is resting on top of a nail head in a stud.

■ Run an electronic stud sensor (available at hardware stores) over the wall. It will make a distinctive sound when it has located a stud.

■ Look for nail heads along the *top* of a baseboard. That's where the baseboard was nailed into a stud.

■ Make the room as dark as possible, then hold a flashlight against the baseboard and aim it straight up the wall. As you slowly move the flashlight along the bottom of the wall, you should see the shadowy imprint of the studs and, in some walls, even glints from nails embedded in the studs.

Very light object
(example: small picture)

Hang a light object on a picture hook, driving a common nail through the angled holes of the hook. Attach wire to the frame with eye hooks. It is stronger to crisscross the wire over two picture hooks than to use a single picture hook.

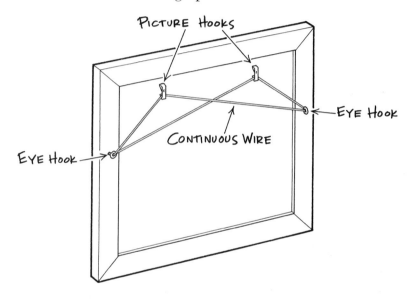

PICTURE HOOKS

EYE HOOK

EYE HOOK

CONTINUOUS WIRE

Light object mounted with screws
(example: rod for short curtains)

Use plastic wall anchors the same size as the screws.

1. Drill a hole that's just big enough to hold the anchor snugly (the package will tell which drill bit to use).

2. Tap the anchor into the hole with a hammer.

3. Run the screw through the screw hole of the item you want to mount, then drive it into the anchor.

Heavier item (examples: shelves, mirror)
Use an expansion anchor, commonly called a
Molly bolt.

1. Drill the recommended size hole in the wall.

2. Tap the bolt into the hole with a hammer and
turn the head clockwise until it's tight. This
indicates that the Molly is secure against the
other side of the wall.

3. Unscrew the bolt, run it through the screw
hole of the item to be mounted, and reinsert it
into the Molly.

*Still heavier items
(example: small cabinet)*
Use toggle bolts.

1. Drill the recommended size of hole in the wall.

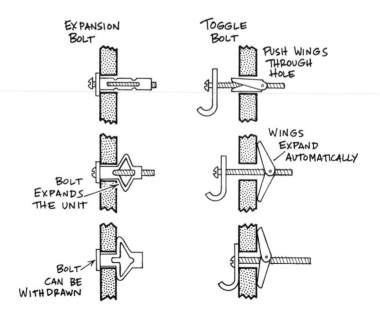

2. Take the flange off the bolt. Run the bolt through the screw hole of the object to be mounted on the wall. Put the flange back on the bolt.

3. Holding the object with one hand, pinch the flange closed with the other hand and push flange into the hole. When the flange is all the way through, pull back on the bolt until you can feel the flange pressing against the inside of the wall. Screw the bolt clockwise until it's tight.

A PLACE FOR BOOKS, TROPHIES, AND TREASURES

Turn a bare wall into a thing of beauty *and* storage space by putting up some shelves. Adjustable shelves have three components: vertical supports called standards, brackets to hold the shelves, and boards.

1. First sketch a design of your shelves. You need to figure out how many shelves, standards, and brackets you'll need and where to place them. Determine the total area that you want to cover with shelving. Consider how many shelves you want in that space and whether you might want to adjust or add shelves in the future. Support a shelve with standards and brackets every 24 inches. No shelf should extend more than 8 inches beyond the outside bracket. You can choose to vary the lengths of the shelves for decorative purposes or to fit around something on or against the wall. Ideally, the standards should be screwed into wall studs (*see* Five Ways to Find a Stud, page 64). If this isn't possible, you can attach a small shelf with Molly bolts (see illustration at left).

2. Once you have a final design, buy the 1-by-10-inch wooden or particleboard shelves, metal standards (plus screws), and brackets. Ask the hardware store if they'll cut the boards for you. If you want to paint, stain, or finish the shelves, do it now so that they're ready to use as soon as the standards and brackets are mounted.

3. Place the left-most standard against the wall over the left-most stud and at the proper height. Make sure the standard is right-end up (check by snapping a bracket in place), then drive in the top screw. With a level, check to see that the standard is vertically plumb before driving in the other screws.

4. Mount the rest of the standards at the exact same height against other wall studs, using a level and precise measurements to determine each position. To check the height, lay your level on the tops of both standards (if your level isn't long enough, put a board on both standards and put the level on top of that).

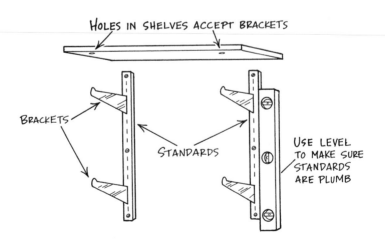

HOLES IN SHELVES ACCEPT BRACKETS

BRACKETS

STANDARDS

USE LEVEL TO MAKE SURE STANDARDS ARE PLUMB

5. Snap the brackets into the standards where you want the shelves, counting holes from the bottom to make sure the brackets are exactly the same height.

6. Mount the shelves on the brackets. Before putting anything on the shelves, push down on them to make sure they're securely in place. Begin filling each shelf from the middle out toward either end, just to make sure that you don't accidentally overload one end and tip the entire shelf.

A DRIER BASEMENT

A damp basement is caused by seepage (water coming in from outside) and/or condensation (water forming from inside humidity). To test for both conditions, tape large squares of aluminum foil to random spots on the basement walls and floor. Run the tape along each side of the square, leaving no gaps for air to get underneath the foil. Two or three days later, remove the tape and examine both sides for moisture: If the inner side is wet, you have seepage; a wet outer side indicates condensation. Once you know the problem, you can to try to solve it:

Seepage
■ Inspect all gutters and down spouts. Make sure that they aren't leaking and that down spouts (if necessary, extended by troughs) empty water at least 8 feet from the foundation.

■ Paint the basement walls and floor with waterproofing paint.

■ Fill in all cracks, holes, and gaps in the basement floors and walls with hydraulic cement.

Condensation

■ Install a dehumdifier or outside fan.

■ Inspect all water pipes for leaks and repair.

■ Wrap all cold-water pipes with pipe insulation.

■ Trim plantings further away from the foundation wall—especially from windows—so more sunlight and circulating air reach it.

True Value Tip

KEEPING PESTS OUT

■ Set up a regular inspection-and-service contract with a local pest control company.
■ Avoid getting indoor pesticides on food, dishes (including pet bowls), and cooking utensils.
■ Make sure children and pets can't come into direct contact with pesticides that are unsafe (consult the label, instruction booklet, or your local pest control professional).
■ Don't store pesticides in the kitchen or other areas where food, dishes, or cooking utensils are kept, and keep them out of reach of children or pets.
■ Vacuum, sweep, and mop floor surfaces regularly and whenever dirty.
■ Store food in pest-safe containers and avoid leaving food out in the open any longer than necessary.
■ Inspect regularly for holes in the walls or foundation and make sure all doors and windows fit snugly in their frames.
■ Inspect your screens for rips and holes.
■ Don't store firewood, birdseed, or large-bulk pet feed inside the house.
■ Keep compost piles and firewood stacks well away from the house.
■ If possible, place patio, deck, or entryway lights on the outer perimeter of these spaces, rather than right against the house.

4 Put on Your Painter's Cap
Painting and Wallpapering

Nothing transforms a room faster and for less money than a fresh coat of paint or new wallpaper. In our stores we hand out buckets of advice to help even first-time painters and paperhangers achieve professional-looking results. Here are the basic techniques, as well as tips that will make the job easier and the results longer-lasting.

Painting Know-how

PICKING PAINT AND TOOLS

Here are tips that will help you pick the best type of paint and the right tools for interior paint jobs:

Latex or alkyd?

■ For most interior surfaces, **latex paint** (water-based paint) is the more practical choice. It dries in just 1 to 2 hours, and you can put on the second coat after 4 hours. You can clean up with just soap and water. Also, you don't have to use an expensive natural-bristle brush.

■ **Alkyd paint** (commonly called oil-based paint, even though it isn't any more) is durable, so it can be a good choice for wooden trim, stair banisters, and rails, or walls from which you expect to be scrubbing dirt or scuff marks. If you want a high-gloss finish for decorative purposes, alkyd paint has a more dramatic sheen than any latex paint. However, alkyd paint has its downsides. It must be applied with brushes made for oil-based paints; has to be cleaned from those brushes with turpentine or mineral spirits; takes 3 to 4 hours to dry, with a recommended 16-hour drying period between coats; and usually costs more than latex paint

Finishes

Latex and alkyd paints come in four finishes.

■ A **flat** or matte finish best hides surface imperfections. It is ideal for ceilings and for walls in formal areas such as living and dining rooms. You can't scrub it, so don't use it in kitchens, bathrooms, and high-traffic areas.

■ An **eggshell** (flat enamel or satin) finish has a slight sheen. Because it resists stains and is easier to clean than flat paint, it's a good compromise for areas where you want both a soft look and some durability.

■ **Semigloss** is a harder, shinier surface than eggshell or satin. Because it's so easy to clean, it's commonly used on woodwork and on the walls of kitchens, bathrooms, and children's rooms.

■ **Gloss**, the hardest and most reflective finish, shows all the surface imperfections, but it resists stains the best and is easiest to clean.

Primers

There are both latex and alkyd primers for undercoating. Primers typically have shorter drying times and broader coverage than the same kind of paint. Any primer will mask marks and colors and bind new paint to the surface. There are also special primers for specific purposes.

■ A **sealing primer** prevents moisture, air leaks, or bleeding from tough stains.

■ A **stain-killing primer** prevents a water or grease stain from bleeding through the new paint.

■ For extra help filling in nicks, scrapes, pockmarks, or pebbly textures, use a **surfacing primer**.

■ If you're working with an especially slick surface (for example: metal, plastic, laminate, or high-gloss finish), use a **bonding primer**.

■ If you're painting over an exceptionally dark color or two or more different colors with a lighter color, use a **hiding primer**.

True Value Tip

THE FIVE MOST-ASKED QUESTIONS ABOUT BUYING PAINT

■ **How much paint should I buy?** A gallon of latex paint covers approximately 350 square feet for a first coat and 400 square feet for a second coat (the second time, paint tends to go on more smoothly, so it goes further). A gallon of alkyd paint covers 400 to 500 square feet.

■ **Do I have to use the same kind of paint that's already there?** It's best to put latex on top of latex, or alkyd on top of alkyd. If you don't know what's there, first cover the old paint with a primer that's the same kind as the new paint.

■ **One coat or two?** Most painting jobs require two coats for an even, thorough, true-color finish. An alkyd flat finish, because of its particularly fine texture, requires only one coat unless you're covering a darker color. Glossy finishes—alkyd or latex—require at least two coats.

■ **What should I put on the ceiling?** For most rooms, a flat, white latex paint is the best choice because it is neutral and diffuses light well. Designated "ceiling paint" serves these purposes and also saves you money because it covers more area than regular latex paint (as it's slightly thinner).

■ **To prime or not to prime?** Apply a coat of primer on bare plaster, wallboard, wood, or masonry surfaces, or on surfaces formerly covered by wallpaper. An underlying primer coat is also advisable if you're covering a darker color with a lighter one, a glossy finish with a flat one, or one kind of paint (alkyd or latex) with the other.

Colors

You can create visual illusions with the colors you choose for a room.

■ Light colors make a room look bigger, cooler, and airier. They also tend to make you feel alert.

■ Dark colors make a room look cozier, warmer, and richer. They tend to make you feel relaxed.

■ A ceiling looks higher when it's painted a lighter color than the surrounding walls, lower when it's painted a darker color.

■ A narrow hallway appears wider when one side is painted a slightly darker shade of the same color that's on the opposite side.

■ To make a long, narrow room look more attractively square, paint the two short sides a darker color than the two long ones.

■ To obscure odd angles in the walls and/or ceiling of a room, paint all walls and the ceiling the same color.

■ To make high walls appear lower, or a cavernous room more intimate, paint the walls in two compatible colors: a darker one on the bottom third and a lighter one on the top two-thirds, with a chair rail between.

True Value Tip

TRUE COLORS

Paint changes color as it dries. To see the actual color of paint, brush a sample onto a paint-stirring stick or other scrap of wood and dry it with a hair dryer or heat gun.

WHICH PAINT DID I USE IN THE HALL?

True Value Tip

When you do touch-ups or repaint an area in the future, you'll need to know what's on the walls and what's inside all those cans on your shelves. Here are various easy ways people have kept track:

■ Before opening a fresh can, cover the instructions and identification labels, numbers, or codes with clear tape so that they won't be accidentally torn off or permanently covered by drips of paint.

■ Keep a log or notebook for writing down the key facts about paint you buy: paint color and brand, any serial or identification number on the can, the room or place being painted, the date of the painting job, and where you purchased the paint.

■ Save a paint stick dipped in the paint so that you can later bring it to a store for matching or for holding next to other colors you're considering for the same room. Write down information about the paint on an unpainted portion of the stick.

■ If you're storing a can with leftover paint inside, attach a masking-tape label that states the date you used it, the room or surface you painted, and where you bought it.

Tools to paint a room

■ You'll need two **brushes**: a 2-inch angular brush for woodwork, windows, and corners, and one 2-inch trim brush for edges and other areas where you'll need extra control. Synthetic bristles

work with both latex and alkyd paint; natural bristles must be used for alkyd paint; foam brushes are good for touch-ups and small jobs. Test brushes before buying them by flexing the bristles and pulling them lightly. They should spring back, not break or stay bent. Don't skimp here. A first-time painter with high-quality brushes can do a better job than a pro with cheap ones.

■ Get a **roller** with a steel frame, a metal cage, and a handle with inside threads that can hold an extension pole. For smooth surfaces, choose a roller cover with a short nap (³⁄₁₆ to ⅜ inch), for rough surfaces, a long nap (¾ to 1¼ inch). There are also narrow rollers for trim and tight areas. A high-quality roller will make a big difference.

■ For your roller, get a **tray**. Metal trays tend to spill less than plastic ones. Tray liners will speed up your cleanup.

■ The most practical **drop cloths** are plastic, either disposable or coated-canvas. Paper tears too easily—and forget about using newspapers!

■ Get a **paint shield** to protect walls while you're doing the woodwork and to help with other edges.

■ **Masking tape** protects unpainted surfaces and holds down your drop cloth. There are now special **painting tapes** with microbarrier edges that reduce bleed-through; they're great for edges or corners where two colors meet.

■ In addition, you'll need paint thinner or solvent (for alkyd paint only), one-sided razor blades,

True Value Tip

To keep the shape of a brush while it's drying and/or stored, cut a long, straight length of coat-hanger wire and run it through the hole in the tip of the paint-brush handle (if no hole exists, drill one before you start painting). Then, hang the wire with strings at each end from a rod, board, or shelf. Place newspapers or rags under the brush to catch drips. When the brush is dry, cover the bristles with a plastic bag tied at the handle and leave the brush hanging from the wire. You can dry and store several brushes on the same length of wire.

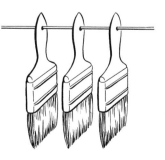

screwdrivers, wall cleaner, cleaning rags, a bucket, and a sponge. You may need a ladder. You'll also need tools for wall preparation, so read the section Preparation Is Everything before making a trip to buy the paint and tools.

True Value Tip

CAN-DO CANS

■ Hate the mess and waste of paint rolling down the outside of the can? As soon as you've removed the lid, punch three or four evenly spaced holes into the rim, being careful not to bend it. Any paint slopped into the rim will drip back down into the can. The seal will be just as tight when the lid is put back on.

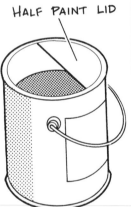

HALF PAINT LID

■ Lloyd Filer, a True Value customer, uses an empty cereal or detergent box as a spill-proof holder for a paint can. Lay the box on one side, trace around the paint can on the other side, and cut out the circle. The paint can will fit snugly and securely inside the hole.

■ You can make a brush wiper and resting place from the lid of an empty paint can. Using a hacksaw or tin snips, cut in half an old lid from a can the same size as you're using on the current painting job. Turn down the cut edge so that its sharpness won't be bothersome. Cover the edge with masking tape, too. When you put the half-lid on the open can you're using, you can strike excess paint off the brush by rubbing it up over the lid edge. You can also rest the brush on the half-lid with the wet bristles hanging over the edge so that paint drips back into the can.

PREPARATION IS EVERYTHING

The better you prepare a room for painting, the better the final results. Never expect paint to cover a surface flaw by itself. Follow this count-down to room readiness:

1. Take out of the room as many pieces of furniture and other stuff as you can. Cover the rest with drop cloths or old sheets.

2. Remove pictures, fixtures, switch and outlet plates, and the hardware on windows and doors. Unscrew ceiling light fixtures so they hang free a bit and you can paint under them. Cover the fixtures with plastic bags.

3. Remove or drive in protruding nails or screws.

4. Scrape off any loose paint or plaster.

5. Fill in small holes, cracks, and nail or screw holes with spackling compound. Allow the spackling compound to dry, then sand. If the hole or crack is large, *see* Chapter 3.

6. Sand down any ridges or bumps.

7. If you're going to paint the edges of a door (the surfaces that fit into the frame), sand off the previous layer(s) of paint. If you don't, the door may stick in the frame after it's painted.

8. If you're painting wooden trim, windows, or doors that already have a glossy finish, lightly roughen the surface with steel wool or very fine sandpaper. If the surface is especially glossy or hard, apply a chemical deglosser (available at hardware stores). Don't put masking tape on the windows: It's easier to paint carefully and scrape off any unwanted paint after it dries.

9. Make sure all surfaces are free of grease spots or other significant stains (*see* Appendix: Super Stain Removal, page 203). If you can't get the stain out, cover it with a stain-killing primer after the washing stage.

10. Lightly dust all surfaces to be painted and clean them with a mixture of water and a low-phosphate household cleaner or with a commercial wall-cleaning product. Washing the walls may seem like a lot of work, but if you skip this step, stains can bleed through or the paint might not hold well, which will ultimately make a lot more work! Allow drying time before painting.

11. Cover the floor with a cloth or plastic drop cloth. Some painters like to stand on a drop cloth that protects the immediate area from drips and then move the same drop cloth along as they work from area to area. Others prefer to cover the entire floor before they begin. If you have carpeting, put painting tape (*see* Tools to paint a room above) against the baseboards, then use regular masking tape to attach the protective cloth to the painting tape.

12. Gather the supplies to wipe up any spills or unwanted paint marks and to clean your hands if necessary. Get rags or paper towels and either a bucket of lightly soapy water (for latex paint) or a can of turpentine or mineral spirits (for alkyd paint).

13. Just before painting, assemble the brushes, roller, roller tray, and other equipment you'll need. Then mix the paint thoroughly with a paint stick. (If you bought the paint weeks or years ago, take it to your hardware store or paint store to be shaken by machine.)

True Value Tip

GETTING READY TO PAINT

■ It's a drag to lose track of screws and other fasteners by the time you're ready to put a lighting fixture or switch plate back on. Next time, as you're removing them, tape them to the back of the fixture and they'll be right where you want them later.

■ Cover all visible wood knots in bare or painted wood with spackling compound, then prime. Left on their own, they soak up paint faster than surrounding wood. Over the years, they'll show up more and more.

■ It's a law of the universe that as soon as you start to paint, someone is sure to interrupt you. Keep handy a pair of old gloves or inexpensive disposable vinyl gloves (or even plastic bags to use as gloves) in case you need to touch something, like a doorknob or telephone, while your hands are covered with paint. Put old sneakers or slippers (ones easy to slip on and off) in a paint-free part of the room and wear them whenever you might track paint across an unprotected floor.

DON'T LOAD UP

True Value Tip

■ When painting with a brush, always load paint only on the bottom third of the bristles. Paint with slow, steady strokes to avoid flinging paint.

■ Fill a roller tray halfway up the incline. Dip the roller into the paint and up onto the incline to slake off excess paint. When you lift up the roller, paint shouldn't drip from it.

PAINTING A ROOM STEP BY STEP

Paint the ceiling first, so drips won't fall on already painted lower surfaces. Walls are second, then trim, doors, and windows. Follow the steps below for each coat of primer or paint. Do all coats on the ceiling before moving to the walls, and so on.

Phase 1: the ceiling

Paint the entire ceiling without stopping for longer than a few minutes. If you apply wet paint over dry paint, you may get streaks.

1. Using a brush or foam pad edger, paint a border 2 to 3 inches wide all along the edge of the ceiling where it meets the walls.

2. Now you're ready to roll. Work in sections about 6 feet square. Make a **W** stroke from right to left, then back from left to right in another **W** to fill in. Finish with overlapping strokes in one direction to blend the paint.

Phase 2: walls

Finish one wall completely before stopping for longer than a few minutes, or you risk making streaks by rolling wet paint over dry paint. Plan ahead so that you don't run out of paint in the middle of a wall. A new batch of same-color paint may not match perfectly, which won't be seen on two different walls but may be obvious on the same wall. Protect the ceiling with painting tape or use an edging tool while you're painting.

1. With a brush or foam pad edger, paint any areas you can't reach with a roller, including the edges of each wall where it meets the floor, other walls, and the ceiling, as well as around any window, door, outlet, switch, wall-fixture, or trim.

2. Roll the wall in a **W** shape (as you did for the ceiling). Finish with strokes from top to bottom.

3. Go on to the next wall.

Phase 3: trim, windows, and doors

Make sure all glossy surfaces have been slightly roughened so the paint will bond (*see* Preparation Is Everything, step 8, above). If you forgot, wait until any wet paint that's nearby has completely dried before doing this. You should also have removed all hardware during the preparation stage.

1. Begin with the upper trim, then do the baseboards. Paint them horizontally with broad, steady strokes, holding a paint shield as you go to keep paint from spilling or spreading onto the floor or the freshly painted wall.

True Value Tip

TOUCH UP
Use a disposable cotton ball to touch up a bare, streaky, or soiled spot while you're painting or afterward.

2. Windows are next. Open the window an inch or two before starting to paint it; if it's double-hung, open both sashes. Begin by painting the window itself, rather than the frame, to reduce the chances you'll bump into wet paint as you go along. On a double-hung window, begin with the top sash. After you've painted the entire window, paint the frame. When you've painted both the window and frame, close the window and paint any spots that you may not have been able to reach when the window was ajar. Later, before the paint on the window has dried, raise it a few inches and lower it again to make sure it won't stick. Don't reinstall window hardware until the paint is completely dry.

3. Paint the doors last. Put a drop cloth under the door. Paint the door first, followed by the frame. If the door is flat, you can save time by using a roller. If the door has panels, you'll need a brush, but you can roll the flat parts with a small roller. Leave the door ajar until it's dry (to keep it from sticking to the frame) and don't reinstall hardware until the paint is completely dry.

Phase 4: cleanup

1. Take up the drop cloths.

2. Clean up any paint spills on the floor or elsewhere, before the paint starts to set. (*see* Appendix: Super Stain Removal, page 207).

3. Clean in this order: brushes, rollers, paint trays, and yourself. If you used **latex paint**, you can do these tasks with warm, soapy water. For brushes, begin by painting or scraping away excess paint, then wash the brushes, massaging them by hand. Run clean water through the washed brushes until it comes out clear. Finally, use a paintbrush comb (available at hardware stores) or a wire brush to make sure the bristles don't dry tangled or stuck together. For paint trays, empty leftover paint into the can and flush the tray with water. For rollers, clean or dispose of the covers and clean the frame and sleeve with a sponge. If you used **alkyd paint**, clean your tools with paint thinner or turpentine and yourself with a strong, abrasive hand cleaner (thinner or turpentine is too harsh for your skin or clothes). Soak brushes in thinner for at least a few minutes. Then, wearing rubber gloves, massage thinner through the brushes and flush with thinner. Repeat until the thinner stays clear. Finally, comb the brushes with a wire brush and shake them dry (preferably outdoors). Dispose of paint tray liners and throw away or clean the roller covers. Clean the carriage and handle with thinner.

4. Scrape any paint drips off the windows with a special scraper, sold for this purpose, that holds a single-edged razor blade.

5. Store leftover paint according to the directions on the paint can. Before disposing of paint, check with your local recycling center. In many communities, environmental laws govern where, when, and how you can discard unwanted paint. Above all, do not pour the paint into the ground or bury it. It's easier and safer to dispose of dried-up paint than wet paint, so if there's a significant amount of wet paint left in the can, add kitty litter, ashes, or dirt to dry it up.

True Value Tip

CLEANING UP YOURSELF
To clean paint from your hands faster, wet them, then put a tablespoon of granulated sugar into one palm and rub your hands together. The sugar will collect the paint. Rinse off the sugary balls of paint and wash as usual.

THE BRUSH-OFF

True Value Tip

■ To hold a brush full of alkyd paint in thinner for cleaning, or for temporarily storing an alkyd-laden brush between painting sessions, attach it to a wooden paint-stick with a rubber band, so that the bristles don't come all the way to the end of the stick. Then insert the stick, with the brush bristle-side down, in a can filled with thinner. The stick will hold the bristles dangling inside the thinner while keeping them from hitting the bottom of the can.

■ Mike Devlin, a True Value dealer in Albany, New York, advises his customers to store their brushes between paintings in small plastic bags. Before sealing or tying the bag, he recommends adding ½ teaspoon of vinegar (for latex paint) or thinner (for alkyd paint) as a moisturizing agent to keep the brush soft and supple for the next job.

■ True Value customer Sandy McCauley puts his brushes in cold storage. When he wants to break for 1 to 4 hours without cleaning brush or roller, he seals it in a plastic bag or

USING A PADDLE TO HOLD A BRUSH IN SOLVENT

aluminum foil and puts it in the refrigerator. It's still wet when the break is over. For longer breaks—up to several days—he stores the sealed brush or roller in the freezer, taking it out an hour or so before reusing to let it thaw.

■ To restore paintbrushes that are stiff from a previous paint job, boil them in white vinegar for 10 to 15 minutes, then gently comb out the old paint with a wire brush.

HOUSE-PAINTING BASICS

In most parts of the country, the exterior of a house is best painted in spring or fall. Hot weather causes paint to dry too fast, before it forms a strong bond. If you do have to paint in the summer, it's best to paint during the cooler hours of early morning and late afternoon.

When you're painting the exterior, you need to plan carefully before you start. What will you paint first, next, last? Take drying times into consideration so you can make the best use of your time.

Once you've decided to launch the project, make sure you have all the necessary ladders, scaffolding, and other equipment (some of which you can rent) on hand, so that you can move quickly and easily as the situation dictates. For information on safety with extension ladders, *see* Chapter 1. Pick days when the humidity is low and no rain is forecast for at least 2 days.

Choosing exterior paint

As a general rule, a primer and two coats of paint are recommended over bare surfaces and two coats of paint over painted ones. If the house was last painted less than 5 years ago, one coat of paint may do, depending on how well the previous paint job has weathered.

When choosing the type of paint (latex or alkyd) and the finish (flat or glossy), consider the following issues:

■ The best kind of paint to use is the same type as the previous layer. If you don't know what was used, latex is the better choice to avoid streaking or peeling.

■ Alkyd paint bonds more strongly but dries more slowly than latex paint, making it more susceptible during drying time to collecting debris and being damaged by unexpected rain.

■ Latex paint not only dries faster but also allows the surface to "breathe" more, which helps reduce moisture problems if you live in a humid climate.

■ Latex paint cleans with water, alkyd with thinner.

■ A flat finish is commonly viewed as the most appropriate for walls and a glossy finish for doors, windows, shutters, and trim.

For coverage and drying times, consult paint can labels and your dealer. These figures vary considerably according to the specific materials you'll be painting. On the average, a gallon of either latex or alkyd exterior paint covers about 400 square feet of painted clapboard and less of other surfaces. Latex dries enough to coat again in approximately 4 hours, alkyd in approximately 24.

Paint colors can create illusions on the exterior of your home

■ To make a small house appear larger, paint it a light color and avoid too much contrast or variety in the trim colors.

■ To make a large, boxy house appear more charming and integrated into its surroundings, paint it a darker color and offer contrast or variety in the trim colors.

■ To give a disproportionately low house more vertical interest, paint the doors, shutters, and corner trim in a significantly lighter or darker color than the rest of the house and trim.

■ To give a disproportionately tall house more horizontal interest, paint the windowsills, window boxes, foundation, and roof-line gutters a significantly lighter or darker color than the rest of the house and trim.

■ To unify a house with a detached garage and other outbuildings, or with several different wings, dormers, or components, paint all walls the same relatively neutral color.

Getting your house ready for a new coat of paint

■ Repair any damaged wood or siding. Scrape away and sand all loose paint.

■ Replace or drive in loose or protruding nails.

■ Caulk around all doors, windows, and joints as necessary to provide good insulation. Allow the caulking to dry before washing or painting.

True Value Tip

PREVENTING MILDEW

In areas with high humidity, mildew often forms on painted areas. You can prevent this by using a commercial mildewcide while painting. Some products are stirred into the paint, others are sprayed on while the paint is still wet.

■ Clean all surfaces. For most dirt, hosing is sufficient.

■ The surfaces must be entirely free from mildew. To remove mildew, scrub it with a commercial mildewcide (available at hardware stores) or a 50/50 bleach-water solution.

■ Paint all bare spots with the primer that's appropriate for the paint you're using (latex or alkyd).

■ Just before painting, protect all surrounding shrubs, plantings, patios, decks, porches, walkways, and driveways by covering them with weighted- or tied-down tarps or sheets.

Painting exterior walls, the basics

■ It's best to complete the entire project as quickly as possible, so that the paint color and texture look uniform from wall to wall and so that dirt doesn't accumulate on surfaces before they're painted. If you plan to paint only one wall at a time with more than a week between walls, give each wall its full number of coats before moving onto the next wall.

■ If practical, begin at the top of the side that's seen least often. This will give you a chance to hone your painting skills before you get to a more "important" side.

■ On each side, paint from the top down so you can cover over drips as you go along. If you find that a drip has hardened, scrape it off before painting over the place. If you're painting with a brush only, cover the broad, unbroken areas first. In each position, begin with horizontal strokes and then make vertical ones to get full coverage with a minimum amount of streaks. (If you're painting clapboard, you'll only be able to make horizontal strokes.) As you go along, fill in borders around windows, doors, and other edges or obstacles *after* you've painted the adjacent broad areas and brush the border paint back into the broad-area paint so that it blends well.

■ If you're painting with a roller, as you go along use a brush or edger to paint borders around windows, doors, and other obstacles *before* you paint the adjacent broad areas with a roller. Start rolling at the uppermost point and go down and back up over the same strip before moving onto the next strip. If you are using a roller on clapboard, you'll only be able to make horizontal strokes. For good blending, strips should overlap above, below, and on either side about 2 to 3 inches.

■ Paint the trim after you've painted the walls.

■ For cleaning your brushes, yourself, and anything else that gets dabbed with unwanted paint, *see* pages 84–86.

True Value Tip

GOOD TRACTION

When you're painting outdoor wooden or masonry surfaces where people will walk, first stir fine sand (sold in hardware stores) into the paint, about 1 part sand to 5 parts paint. After the mixture dries, it will have a gritty texture, providing good traction even when it's wet. Stir the mixture frequently while you're painting to keep the sand evenly distributed.

Wallpapering Know-how

WHAT TO BUY

Whenever wallpapering, first consult with a dealer to find out which specific papering procedures and equipment are likely to work best for the paper you're using and the surface you're covering.

Your options

■ **Self-adhesive or paste yourself?** Prepasted papers may eliminate the need for additional pasting altogether. Typically the paper is put into a water tank to activate the paste, then unrolled and applied to the wall. This kind of wall covering can be much quicker, easier, and cleaner to use than the kind you paste yourself. However, you have to be careful to soak the paper properly so that the paste isn't too dry or too wet. Also, if you're working on a rough or porous wall, there may not be enough paste on the paper to form a tight bond; you'll have to supplement it by applying more of the same type of paste, which means keeping a bucket of paste and a brush on hand.

■ **Coated or backed vinyl?** The most common kind of wallpaper is vinyl-coated, which works fine under most circumstances. If the room or your local climate has high humidity, a paper- or cloth-backed vinyl will be more durable. These two types are also more traffic-resistant, but, being heavier, they're slightly more cumbersome to apply and require a bit more adhesive per square foot.

■ **Foil, wet-look, or fibrous covering?** Foil covering or wet-look vinyl covering is attractive and appropriate in areas that often get an extra dose of humidity and will benefit from a lot of light reflection, such as kitchens, bathrooms, and laundry rooms. Fibrous covering (such as burlap or grass cloth) should only be used in rooms that are dry and won't get as much traffic. All of these fancier coverings have to be applied on top of lining paper so there are two papering processes involved.

■ **Patterns or stripes?** Some patterns and stripes are more difficult to match up when you're hanging them. You may have to trim sheets so they match up well (for example, so that there is the right space between stripes or so that two halves of an image meet). If the design is fairly complicated, you may need to buy as much as 25 percent more paper. As a general rule, small prints make a room look larger, while large prints make it look smaller. Vertical stripes add height to the walls of a room, while horizontal stripes add width.

How much to buy?

To figure out how many rolls of wallpaper you'll need, measure the total square footage of the wall space. If you will be covering all the walls in a room, multiply the room's width by length by height, then deduct the square footage of the doors and windows. Most single rolls of wallpaper contain about 36 square feet of paper, regardless of the length or width of the paper (for example, a roll 24 inches wide will be about 18 feet long; a roll 27 inches wide will be about 16 feet long). However, the actual yield of a wallpaper roll is closer to 30 square feet because of trimming and waste. Your dealer can confirm how much paper you need.

The basic tools for wallpapering are a brush, utility knife, ruler, smoothing sponge, seam roller, drop cloths, pasting table (*see* Getting the Room Ready; step 8, below), and (if you're not using self-adhesive paper) paste. The right brush and paste depends upon the wallpaper you choose, so consult your dealer.

GETTING THE ROOM READY

1. Take out of the room as many pieces of furniture and other objects as you can. Move any remaining items to the center of the room where they'll be out of the way. Lay drop cloths around the perimeter of the room to catch paste drips or dropped strips.

2. Take down pictures, hanging items, fixtures, and switch or outlet plates.

3. Remove or drive in protruding nails or screws.

4. *If the surface is already covered with paper in good condition* (tight, level, applied properly), you may be able to paper on top of the old wallpaper. If you find a few loose spots or bumps, try to reseal them. Otherwise, cut or scrape them away, feathering the edges. The walls should then be covered with sizing, a glue that will keep the old paper from absorbing too much wallpaper paste. For the best surface, though, you should remove the paper.

5. *If the existing paper is not in good condition* (lots of loose spots, bumps, or gaps), if there are more than two layers of old paper, or if you want to have the best possible surface for the new paper, you should remove all the old paper with a chemical solution or a steamer, followed by a good scraping and, finally, a scrub down with a heavy detergent to get rid of all old adhesive. The walls should then be covered with the appropriate sizing.

6. *If the surface to be covered is bare wallboard, plaster, or wood*, it should first be coated with the appropriate sizing. Ask your dealer what type to use.

7. *If the surface is covered with paint*, make sure it is clean and even. Sand away bumps, ridges, and loose paint. Remove or drive in any protruding nails or screws. Smoothly spackle over these spots as well as any cracks or depressions. Also spackle smoothly over stains you can't remove. In most cases, the wall won't require a coat of sizing before papering; consult your dealer to make sure.

8. If you're not using self-adhesive paper, set up a table where you will paste the backs of new wallpaper strips: preferably one that can get messy, such as a sheet of plywood laid on two sawhorses or a table protected by a sheet.

WALLPAPERING BASICS

If you're using wallpaper that is *not* self-adhesive, follow the steps below. For self-adhesive wallpaper, follow the guidelines that accompany the paper or consult a dealer.

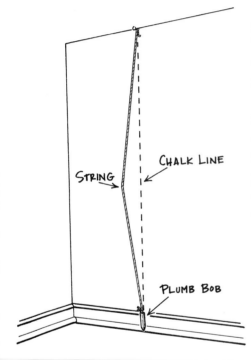

1. Begin in the least viewed corner of the room. Save the more "important" corners for later, when you'll have developed a rhythm.

2. At the top of the wall, measure out a horizontal distance about 1 inch narrower than the width of your paper. At this place, tack in a chalked plumb line (or a chalk-covered string with a plumb or small weight at the end) that reaches almost to the floor. Hold the plumb line taut against the bottom of the wall and snap it. This will make a perfectly perpendicular chalk guideline on the wall for the first strip of paper.

3. Using a utility knife against a ruler, cut the first strip of paper about 4 inches longer than the wall is high. Lay the strip face down on the pasting table. Brush paste onto the top half of the strip and then, without pressing, gently fold the pasted section down so the pasted sides are together. Follow the same pasting-and-booking procedure on the lower half of the strip. This is a folding technique called booking that makes the strip temporarily shorter for easier handling. Let the strip sit for 5 to 10 minutes before hanging, to cure.

4. Carry the folded strip over to the corner of the wall where you're beginning. Unfold the top half of the strip and lay it against the wall so that the top edge of the paper juts about 2 inches beyond the top of the wall and one side of the paper is perfectly aligned with the plumb line (making the other side slightly overlap the corner). Smooth out this half of the strip with your hand, working toward the corner of the wall. Smooth the side of the strip around the corner and onto the other wall. Unfold the bottom half of the strip and smooth it out the same way. It will jut slightly beyond the bottom of the wall and, like the top half, overlap the corner.

5. Using a smoothing brush or a large sponge, go over the entire strip to make sure it adheres tightly to the wall. Force out bubbles and excess paste, and, as a final touch, press or even pound firmly along all edges and the corner. Leave the excess paper untrimmed until *after* applying the next strip.

6. Cut, paste, and book the next strip. *Note:* If you're applying paper with a pattern, before you cut this strip make sure that it will match the previous one when applied. You may need to adjust the paper by a few inches before cutting.

7. Hang the second strip so that it butts right against the edge of the first strip that didn't go around the corner. Slide the second strip in place (rather than pulling it) so that there's virtually no gap between the two strips. After you've hung the second strip, go back and trim all excess paper off the top and bottom of the first strip by running a utility knife along a ruler. After this trimming, run a seam roller along the seam between the first and second strip to seal it in place.

8. Continue hanging strips around the room without leaving any gaps. When hanging a strip over a window or door, smooth the strip all the way to the frame of the door or window, crease it well, and cut it roughly to fit (on the larger side, not smaller). Later, when you're trimming the rest of the strip, you can also trim the edge around the frame.

True Value Tip

FIXING A RIP OR HOLE IN YOUR WALLPAPER

■ If you can't simply glue the paper back in place, you can make a practically invisible patch. First, pull out your stash of extra paper (ideally kept in an out-of-the-way place where it's exposed to a similar amount of sunlight to allow for similar fading). From this stash, carefully tear out a section that will cover the rip or hole, leaving as little overlap as possible. Then paste it in place, feathering the edges of the patch into the surrounding paper. Because of the patch's ragged edges, it will blend in better with the rest of the paper than a patch that's been clean-cut with scissors.

■ If a seam between two strips of wallpaper has curled, glue it back in place. If the paper has shrunk so that the two strips no longer fit together, you can try patching the space between (see above), but often the gap will still be detectable because of the length of the seam edges. In such cases, it's time to re-paper!

⑤ Open and Shut Cases
Windows and Doors

It seems that windows and doors are always sticking, dragging, leaking, wobbling, even falling apart. That's because they're the moving parts of your house, and they get far more use than you realize. After years of up and down, in and out, they need some attention. Damage can also happen instantly, if something smashes a window or rips a screen. As long as you have this chapter handy, no problem!

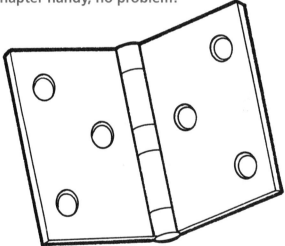

Emergency

BROKEN LOCK

Any trouble with a lock should be considered an emergency—it can easily become a security risk and even keep you out of your own home.

When a key breaks, or an object gets stuck, in the lock

If you're locked out and the key went all the way in before it broke, try turning the key with a pair of pliers. If that doesn't work, try to remove the broken piece or object with pliers or with a thin, rigid wire, hat pin, or a key extractor (available at hardware stores). If this fails and it's possible to get on the other side of the door, unscrew and pull out the lock cylinder and push the broken key or object back out with a thin, rigid wire, hat pin, or key extractor. If this isn't possible or doesn't work, call a locksmith.

When the lock is frozen

Melt frozen moisture inside the lock by heating the key with a flame and then inserting it carefully into the lock, by spraying the keyhole with a lock de-icer (available at hardware stores), or by blowing the lock with a hair dryer.

When the lock won't move, or is hard to move, after you've inserted the key

The interior lock probably needs cleaning and lubricating. Remove it from the door, wash it in a petroleum solvent (available at hardware stores), and apply a small amount of penetrating oil (also available at hardware stores) to all visible moving parts before reinserting it. Never apply oil to the keyhole itself; only use graphite there.

When the key won't insert smoothly
Rub lubricating graphite back and forth across
the key teeth and reinsert the key in the lock.

*When the key turns but won't
activate the lock*
The lock is broken and it's probably best to call
a locksmith to repair or replace it, unless you
feel capable of replacing the lock yourself, using
a kit from your hardware store.

*When the bolt doesn't catch in the strike
plate unless you jiggle the door, or it
doesn't catch well enough to stay*
The door probably needs to be realigned (*see*
All the Right Moves for Doors below). You may
also need to move the strike plate so the latch
goes squarely into the hole: raising the plate,
lowering it, pulling it forward by putting a shim
behind it, or chiseling out space behind it.

Know-how

NO-PAIN PANE REPLACEMENT
It's the stuff of cartoons. A high-flying baseball, a
low-flung elbow, or a mad cross-sweep of a
broom, and *crash!* Where there was once a window, there's now only the wind. You can replace a
pane easily and expertly by following these steps:

1. Wearing work gloves to protect your hands,
remove the old glass from the frame. Pieces
that are embedded in the frame are most safely
removed by wiggling them until they come
loose. However, it may be necessary to knock
pieces out with a hammer and then pry any

remaining glass fragments from the frame with an awl or screwdriver.

2. Scrape all the old putty from the frame. If the putty is too hard, first apply linseed oil and let it soak in until the putty softens. When scraping a *wooden* frame, save the small metal tabs (known as glazier's points) that you encounter (or buy a new package); when scraping a *metal* frame, save the spring clips (if you lose them or they're damaged, you'll have to replace them).

3. Scour all remaining traces of old putty from the frame with a wire brush, steel wool, or sandpaper.

4. If the frame is made of wood, coat the newly exposed wood with linseed oil.

5. Measure the frame for the new pane, subtracting $\frac{1}{16}$ to $\frac{1}{8}$ inch from each side to allow for eventual expansion and contraction of the glass. Have your hardware store cut the new pane.

6. Roll a fistful of putty (or glazing compound) between your hands until it forms a long string the width of a pencil. Press the snake all along the edge of the frame against which you'll be pushing the new glass.

7. Insert the new pane of glass and push it against the putty so that it's firmly in place. Any putty that squeezes out of the frame can be removed in the last step.

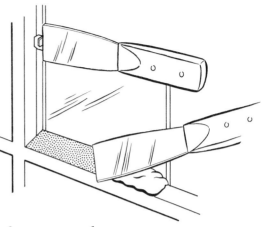

8. Hold the pane against the putty in the frame with points or clips. For a wooden frame, every 8 inches push a glazier's point part way into the wood between the glass and the frame, using the blade of your putty knife. For a metal window, snap the spring clips into the existing holes.

9. To secure the outside of the pane, apply small dabs of putty all around the pane where it meets the frame. Using a putty knife, smooth it against the frame and the pane so that it looks like the putty in the other frames.

10. With a wet cloth, clean excess putty from both sides of the window and the frame. Allow it to dry for 4 days before painting.

DUCT TAPE TO THE RESCUE AGAIN

True Value Tip

Jerry Hinds, a True Value customer, always follows this clean, safe procedure for tapping out a broken windowpane. First, he covers both sides of the pane with cross-strips of duct tape, being careful not to extend the tape beyond the pane. Then, starting at the right- or left-hand edge of one side of the pane, he runs a strip of tape across the middle of the pane and extends it onto the neighboring frame or pane. Finally, he hammers gently all around the edges of the pane until it comes free as a unit. The tape extension keeps the pane from falling and serves as a handle for carrying it away.

PUTTY TRICKS

True Value Tip

- If you lightly coat your putty knife with linseed oil or water, putty won't stick to the blade. If you oil it afterward, too, the knife won't rust.
- Puttying around windowpanes—and many other places, for that matter—requires a lot of blade scraping so that the application is smooth and the surrounding area isn't blotched with spillover. Gene Perrault made a perfect blade-scraper and putty-saver based on directions given to him by his local True Value dealer. In an old putty can, he cut a slit wider and thicker than his knife blade. Whenever he wants to clean his knife blade, all he has to do is run it through the slit, scraping along the edges, and the excess putty drops neatly into the can for reuse.

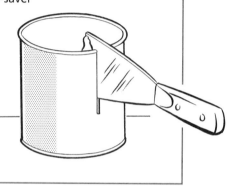

A STUBBORN WINDOW

Resist the temptation to jerk a sticky or stuck window open or closed. You won't do anything except hurt your back. Instead, try these steps to get things moving again:

1. Examine the connection between window and frame all around for sections that might be sealed shut with paint or an adhesive. Insert a putty knife into suspected sections (which may be the entire perimeter) and try to wriggle the window free from the frame. If that doesn't work, lightly tap the putty knife with a hammer until you can get it between the window and the frame. If the window still won't move, check the other side to make sure that it, too, hasn't been painted or bonded to the frame.

2. If the window isn't painted or bonded to the frame on either side but still won't move, the problem may be overly thick paint on the tracks along which the window is meant to slide. Remove this paint by sanding, scraping with a rasp, or lightly chiseling. Then lubricate the track by running a bar of soap back and forth across it or by coating it with a silicone spray.

3. If the window still won't move, try opening it (ideally from the outside) with a small pry bar, using a small piece of wood under the bar for leverage.

4. If the window still won't move, try to free the sash from the frame by tapping the frame away from the window. Put a 2 x 4 along the sash and tap against it with a hammer.

5. If the window *still* won't move, try any or all of these steps again.

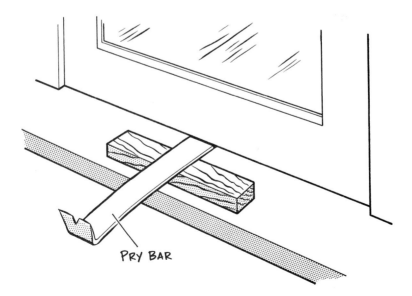

PRY BAR

WINDOWS OF OPPORTUNITY

True Value Tip

■ To make sure you always know which screens and storm windows go in which windows, do what Kay Brockton's True Value dealer advised her to do: Mark them with coded staples. Use a staple gun to mark each window-storm-and-screen set with its own number of lines (staples): one staple for the first group, two staples for the second, etc. For a fancy touch, use Roman numerals.

■ Cook up your own solution for removing paint, plaster, grime, or pollution from door, window, or shutter hinges, handles, and other hardware. Put the hardware in a pan filled with a solution of 4 tablespoons of baking soda per 1 quart of cold water. Heat the water slowly on a burner until it reaches a simmer. After 20 minutes, take out the hardware and scrub it with steel wool to remove any particles that remain. Repeat if necessary.

■ If your window rattles when the wind blows (sometimes this happens despite weather stripping), apply same-color waterproof tape inside the casing so that the sash presses against it. If one layer doesn't work, try two or even three. It should stop the rattle cold.

SCREEN SAVING

The first rule for mending any wire screen that's been punctured, ripped, or blasted through is to take care of it as soon as you notice the damage. Left untreated, the hole will get bigger.

To fix a tiny puncture

Use a small pick, awl, scissor prong, or other pointed tool to restore individual strands of wire to their rightful positions. Then dab the formerly punctured area with clear nail polish or shellac. You may have to apply several coats, letting each one dry before adding the next, before the area is securely covered.

To fix a rip

Move strands of wire back in place with a pointed tool. Then sew the rip shut by stitching back and forth with a similar piece of wire or a nylon thread that's the same color. To make the sewn area even more secure, apply several coats of clear nail polish or shellac, letting each one dry before the next one is added.

To fix a hole

In four easy steps, you can make a nearly invisible patch for a small hole in a window or door screen with a scrap piece of screen and a small amount of clear, silicone caulking:

1. Trim the hole so that the edges are even and flat.

2. Cut a scrap patch in the same shape all around, only slightly larger.

3. Apply the caulking lightly to all edges of the patch and fit it over the hole; the caulking will automatically form an adhesive bond between the two screens.

4. Gently wipe off any excess caulking with a clean rag and allow a couple days for complete drying.

ALL THE RIGHT MOVES FOR DOORS

If a door sticks, drags, or won't shut completely, there are several possible causes. The door may not have been installed correctly, the hinges may have worked loose from the frame, the wood may have swollen or warped, or the house may have settled causing the frame to move.

Try me first

First, make sure the hinge pins are completely in place; if one is sticking out, push it down with your fingers or tap with a hammer. Next, tighten the screws fastening the hinges to the door frame. If a screw won't tighten, remove it, insert one or more wooden matchsticks or toothpicks into the hole to make it smaller, and reinsert the screw. See if tightening the screws has cleared up the door problem. If it hasn't, maybe the jamb is just swollen. Try placing a flat piece of wood against the jam and hitting it with a hammer where the door is sticking. If this doesn't fix the problem, go to the next steps below.

Smoothing the sticking points

■ Carefully examine all around the edges of the door for points where it sticks in the frame. Sometimes you'll see a shiny spot there. Also try slowly opening and closing the door and observing precisely where it sticks. As a last resort, cover the door edge with chalk, then open and close the door one time; the chalk will have been rubbed from the sticking points. However you find the sticking spots, mark them with chalk or another washable marker.

■ If there are only small sticking points here and there, try sanding them off, being careful not to sand too much off or the door won't fit tightly.

■ If the sticking points are too broad or deep to just sand off, you'll have to remove the door to fix it. Start with the bottom hinge. Tap out the hinge pin from underneath with a nail or nail set and a hammer. Then move on to the top hinge, being ready to grab the door quickly if it should start falling as soon as the hinge pin is removed. It's good to have a helper here. (Later, when you're putting the door back, reverse the process. Align the leaves of both hinges, insert the pin in the top hinge, then do the bottom one.)

■ If the door sticks in broad areas at the top, bottom, and/or sides, shave down the sticking points with a wood plane and coarse sandpaper.

If the door sags so the latch side is too low
If the top and bottom corners of the latch side of the door are hanging too low, you can correct the sagging door by moving the bottom hinge out, digging the top hinge farther into the frame, or sometimes both.

■ To move the bottom hinge out, put a shim (a thin piece of material to create extra thickness; a matchbook cover may do it) between the hinge and the door. Unscrew the hinge from the door and use the flat part as a model to cut out a same-size piece of noncompressible cardboard, particleboard, or sheet metal (sheet brass, the strongest material, is sold in various shim sizes at

True Value Tip

SELF-SANDING DOOR

If the bottom edge of a door sticks against the floor, you may be able to sand it down without taking the door off its hinges. Vince Pucci learned this trick from his True Value dealer: Tape a piece of sandpaper to the floor, grit-side up, at the place where the door sticks. Then briskly move the door back and forth across it, and it will sand itself! To keep the process going strong, elevate the sandpaper with thin sheets of cardboard as the edge sands away.

hardware stores). Mark screw holes in the shim and punch them out with a hammer and nail. Then, laying down the shim first followed by the hinge leaf, screw the hinge back on the door.

■ The problem might also, or alternatively, be a top door hinge leaf that is not set deeply enough into the door. The recessed setting is called a mortise. Pressed firmly into its mortise, the hinge leaf should be flush with the door and no higher. If the leaf is higher, the mortise needs to be cut deeper. Unscrew the hinge leaf from the door. Hand-chisel the mortise to a lower depth, angling the chisel as flat (parallel to the door edge) as you can and stroking from several different directions to achieve a level, smooth surface, including in the corners. Check the depth frequently by putting the hinge back, so you won't cut so deeply that the leaf won't sit flush with the door.

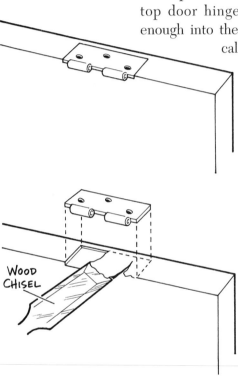

WOOD
CHISEL

If the door sags so the latch side is too high

■ Put a shim under the top hinge, between the hinge leaf and the door. *See* above.

■ The problem might also, or alternatively, be a bottom door hinge leaf that needs to be set deeper into the door. *See* above.

MISBEHAVING DOORS

■ Got a door that bangs shut every now and then, scaring the wits out of everyone inside? Muffle the noise with a line of adhesive-backed weather stripping pressed into the frame where the door hits it. If the stripping is too wide to allow the door to latch, try ⅛-inch foam pads that you can cut into small tabs and glue to three or four places along the frame.

■ To keep a swinging door from opening or shutting too freely, Leanne Weatherby follows a secret she learned from her local True Value dealer. She takes the pin out of the top hinge, wraps it once around with cellophane tape, and reinserts it. This tiny bit of cushioning makes the door move a little more slowly but just as smoothly.

■ Sometimes an interior door latch that gets a lot of use becomes wobbly. This is an especially common problem with bathroom door latches that are repeatedly locked and unlocked. The trouble is that the screws no longer fit snugly in their enlarged holes. The solution to the problem is either to replace the screws with longer ones or to take out each screw, insert a wooden match or small sliver of wood into its hole, and drive the screw into the hole so that it bites into the extra wood.

A SLIDING DOOR THAT WON'T SLIDE

For a sliding door that balks or won't move at all, True Value dealers offer these tips:

■ Often the problem is a low-riding door that binds in the bottom track. Check any and all brackets at the top of the door. Tighten all screws by turning them clockwise. This may lift the door enough to make it ride smoothly again.

■ Check any and all screws in the bottom and top tracks to make sure they're tight.

■ Spray WD-40 along the top and bottom tracks to see if that improves the ride. You can also try a graphite spray, but graphite is more likely to clog.

■ As a final resort, check the surrounding wooden frame to see whether it's out of line anywhere. If so, the doors will have to be removed and the frame problem corrected before the doors will operate smoothly.

DODGING THE DRAFT: WINDOWS

As you gaze out your window, do you feel a draft? In the winter, cold air goes in and warm air goes out. In the summer, it's the opposite. To stop this energy drain around wooden-frame windows, you need to weather-strip from time to time.

If you have metal-frame windows, the manufacturer has built in insulation. If this insulation breaks down, it has to be replaced with identical material by a professional glazier.

What and when to weather-strip

You may be able to identify specific leaks in a window by running a hair dryer around the perimeter while someone outside feels for leaks or, during the winter months, by looking for condensation or frost on the pane (especially common between a double-hung sash window and a storm window). However, it's best to weather-strip *all* windows just to be certain and to replace weather stripping whenever it looks worn or noticeably fails to make a seal. Unfortunately, no weather stripping works forever.

Choosing weather-stripping materials

For most windows, especially double-hung sash and casement windows, vinyl weather stripping works best. The insulating portion can be a tube, foam, felt, or sponge. The vinyl is easier to install than the metal type, and it lasts longer and seals better than the compressible-strip type. Some kinds have adhesive backing and others are attached with brads. Unfortunately, the vinyl stuff is the most visible kind of weather stripping, and if painted, it loses some of its effectiveness.

Compressible-strip weather proofing, made of foam, felt, or rubber, is designed to insulate spaces between a window casement stop and the corresponding sash. It's not much help in sealing the cracks along which a window sash slides or the space between double-hung window sashes, although the packaging may include installation instructions for those purposes.

Metal weather stripping comes in a variety of mostly spring-style configurations. Like compressible-strip weatherproofing, it's used to seal spaces between a window casement stop and the corresponding sash. It's much more difficult to install but far more durable.

Installing vinyl weather stripping

These instructions are for a double-hung sash window, but you can easily adapt them for other kinds of windows. Vinyl insulation is installed on the outside of the window.

1. Measure the height and width of each window and cut all the strips mentioned in the steps below *before* beginning the installation. This tells you whether you have enough material and streamlines the installation. If you're working on a ladder, it also saves you trips up and down.

2. On a double-hung sash window, begin with vertical strips of insulation for the lower sash. Place a strip so that the insulating part (tube, foam, etc.) presses gently against the sash. Every 2 to 3 inches, attach the strip by nailing in a brad.

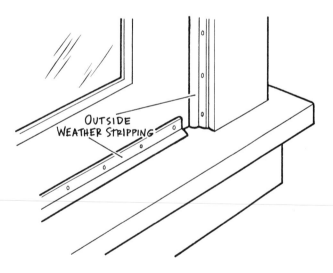

3. Still working on the lower sash, attach a horizontal strip of insulation to the outside surface of the bottom rail so that the insulating part presses gently against the sill.

4. Moving to the upper sash, attach the vertical strips as you did for the lower sash in step 2. Next, attach a horizontal strip to the underside of the bottom rail so that it presses gently against the lower sash.

5. Finally, attach a horizontal strip to the upper sash's top rail so that it presses gently against the frame.

Installing a compressible strip

Attach the stripping to the bottoms of the window (the casement stop molding) rather than to the sashes themselves. If the strip is not self-adhesive, use brads, spaced 2 to 3 inches apart.

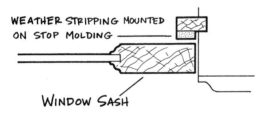

WEATHER STRIPPING MOUNTED ON STOP MOLDING

WINDOW SASH

Installing metal weather stripping

Follow the package instructions carefully or consult your hardware dealer.

True Value Tip

TOTAL WEATHER- STRIPPING

When weather- stripping doors and windows, don't forget to include these often over- looked sources of drafts:

• a door leading to an unheated room, crawl space, porch, or garage
• an air-conditioning unit installed in a window
• an attic door
• pull-down stairs
• all garage doors and windows

DODGING THE DRAFT: DOORS

Like windows, outside doors need to be dressed properly to ensure that the weather doesn't pass right through them. Inside doors to unheated spaces like basements, garages, and attics should be weathertight, too. Check the effec- tiveness of your insulation by running a hair dryer around the door perimeter while some- one stands on the other side, following your motions and feeling for leaks.

If the door is leaking at the bottom, install a springy metal or vinyl strip at the bottom. For the top and sides, install foam weather stripping with an adhesive backing.

Installing foam weather stripping

1. Clean the inside of the door jamb (where the edge of the door fits when closed) and allow it to dry thoroughly.

2. Measure and cut the amount of stripping you'll need to go up one side, across the top, and down the other side (three separate strips). (Not the bottom, as leaks there are better stopped with a metal or vinyl strip).

3. Apply each strip to the inside of the door jamb so that the door will close against it. Make sure there are no gaps (you can fill them with small pieces of stripping).

❻ Waterworks
Your Plumbing System

Like many home owners, you may have occasional bouts of aquaeducphobia, or fear of plumbing. In fact, plumbing is a reasonable thing to worry about, since any problem can quickly spell (or is it spill?) disaster. That's why you need to know what to do in case of an emergency. It's also why it pays to take good care of your plumbing system. Don't let aquaeducphobia keep you from handling emergencies or basic maintenance tasks yourself. When it's time to install or replace a pipe or fixture, however, most people should call a plumber.

True Value Tip

BASIC PLUMBING TOOLS

Here are the tools to have on hand for the most common plumbing maintenance and repair tasks. If you keep them together, in a separate toolbox, you'll be able to grab everything you need quickly in a plumbing emergency.

■ Every home needs an 18-inch **plunger** or "plumber's friend." Choose one with a simple force cup; models with an interior cone may not work on sinks. Good plungers are rigid and thick.

■ Buy a flexible **snake** (also called an auger) for cranking through clogs in drains and pipes. Get a good one, since low-quality snakes can kink when you reach a turn in the pipe. Choose a model with a container to hold the dirty snake wire.

■ Get two **pipe wrenches**: a 10-inch and an 18-inch. It's also good to have a 10-inch **adjustable wrench** (*see* Chapter 1).

■ In addition to the sets of Phillips and slotted screwdrivers that are part of your general tool collection, it's useful to have a set of **offset screwdrivers** so you can reach screw heads at odd angles.

■ A **valve-seating tool** removes corrosion from the valve seats of faucets.

■ For timely replacements, buy a bag or box of assorted **washers**, **screws**, and **O-rings** in different sizes.

■ Buy a package of **faucet nut packing** for securing and leakproofing faucet nuts.

■ Buy two or three rolls of **electrician's tape** to wrap around pipes that have small leaks. This will usually stop the leak temporarily until a better repair can be made. Other items to keep on hand for emergency leak repairs are **epoxy putty**, **C-clamps** in various sizes, and **rubber sheeting** (to make small pieces of rubber sealing for leaks).

■ For sealing or resealing pipe threads, buy **pipe tape** (easier and quicker to use than joint compound and better for this purpose than petroleum jelly).

Emergencies

True Value Tip

BEFORE AN EMERGENCY HAPPENS, GET TO KNOW YOUR SYSTEM

You will save precious time and energy during a plumbing emergency if you are familiar with all the pipes, shutoffs, meters, and drains in the system. It is especially critical to know where the main shutoff is for the whole house. Draw a chart showing what is what and how to get to it. Clearly label exposed pipes so that you know whether they carry hot or cold water. Mark shutoffs so they are easily visible and anyone can tell how to work them. If you need help figuring out this information, call your water supplier or a local building inspector and ask for advice.

CLOGGED DRAIN

To unclog a drain in a sink, tub, or toilet bowl, start with the simplest approach, a plunger; if that doesn't work, go on to the other methods until you unclog the drain.

If a toilet bowl is overflowing, first stop the flow of water into the toilet by turning the shutoff valve. Clean up the worst of the mess and then follow the steps until you unclog it.

Using a plunger

1. If there's no water in the sink, tub, or toilet bowl, fill it with about 2 inches of water. Also, if

there's an overflow drain near the rim of the sink, tub, or bowl, stuff it with a wet cloth. These steps will strengthen the suction.

2. Slowly put the plunger into the water *at an angle* so the bell will wind up holding water rather than air.

3. Position the bell over the drain, with the rim of the bell touching the sink, tub, or bowl surface all the way around, and quickly but firmly work the plunger up and down about 15 times.

4. If there doesn't seem to be enough suction, coat the rim of the bell with petroleum jelly and repeat.

5. Run hot water through the pipe to break through any remaining clog.

6. If this doesn't clear up the clog, go to the next level and clean out the trap (*see* below). (You can also try chemical drain cleaners, but they're not recommended if you have cast-iron or steel pipes in your plumbing system or if you have a septic system.)

Cleaning out the trap

If plunging doesn't work, remove the clean-out plug at the bottom of the trap:

1. First put on rubber gloves and place a bucket under the plug.

2. Unscrew the plug with a pipe wrench and allow any water or other matter to drain into the bucket.

3. Using a coat-hanger wire or a similar probe, clean out any remaining clog matter into the bucket.

4. When the trap seems clear, screw the plug back in and run hot water through the pipe. If there's still a block, it's farther along in the pipe. Next, try a snake.

Using a plumber's snake

If the methods above don't do the trick, the problem is somewhere beyond the trap. A plumber's snake is the tool for this job.

1. Remove the clean-out plug (*see* above).

2. Push a snake into the trap and beyond as far as it will go. Then turn it by rotating the handle.

3. If the snake stops moving, give it a hard push while rotating the handle. If it still won't move, slowly pull it out a bit and then try moving it forward again by pushing and turning the handle. If the snake continues to stop at a point, it's probably gone as far as it can, so pull it slowly all the way out.

4. Screw in the clean-out plug and run hot water through the pipe. If you're still clogged up, it's time to call a plumber or drain and sewer cleaner.

ANTI-CLOG STRATEGIES

■ You *may* be able to melt your troubles away. Many clogs are caused by too much grease caught in the trap or slightly beyond. Before getting out the snake, try heating that area with a hair dryer. If grease is causing the clog, the heat will melt the grease, and you can flush it out with hot water.

■ If a plunger handle wobbles or even pulls out when you're suctioning, bind the handle more tightly to the cup with an adjustable automobile hose clamp.

■ Keep clogs from forming in sink, shower, and bathtub drains by installing filters or screens that allow water to pass but trap hair, dirt, and other stuff.

BREAD ON THE WATER

Kevin Dixon, a True Value dealer in Corvallis, Oregon, recommends this trick to keep water from leaking down a copper pipe while you're soldering it. Roll up a tight ball of unseeded bread and push it into the pipe so it's blocked. When you have finished soldering, simply turn the water back on and the bread will dissolve.

TEMPORARY PATCHES FOR A LEAKY PIPE

When a pipe springs a leak, first turn off the valve supplying water to the pipe. As soon as possible, have a plumber replace the pipe or, if you feel confident about doing so, replace it yourself. If it will be several days or weeks until the pipe can be replaced, you can make a temporary patch. Here are some options, beginning with the most effective patch:

■ Wrap a single thickness of rubber around the leaky part of the pipe and hold it in place with a tightly screwed sleeve clamp of the exact same diameter.

■ Over a pinhole leak, apply a piece of rubber and hold it in place with a tight hose clamp (an auto hose clamp works well).

■ Wrap a pinhole leak on a relatively small pipe (copper or PVC) with electrical tape, overlapping each turn and covering the pipe with four layers for 3 to 4 inches on either side of the leak.

■ When the leak is on a fitting or joint that can't be clamped or tightly wrapped with tape, you can make a patch from epoxy putty. First make sure the pipe surface is completely dry. Then apply epoxy putty in several thin layers all over and around the area where leakage is suspected, allowing each layer to dry before applying the next one.

EPOXY
ON PIPE JOINT

FROZEN PIPE

If water doesn't come out of a faucet during freezing weather, then a pipe is probably frozen. Leave the faucet open and try to locate the section of pipe. If the pipe has burst, you'll see water; turn off the water and call a plumber to replace that section and to inspect the entire run for possible weak spots.

If the pipe hasn't burst, you may be able to thaw it out on your own (plumbers do this, too). First, locate the frozen pipe by touch—it will be noticeably colder than the rest of the run. If

you can't find the frozen section, you'll have to start thawing at the beginning of the run and keep going until water finally comes out of the faucet. Here are your options for thawing out the frozen pipe:

■ Apply a heat lamp or a towel saturated with boiling water to the pipe until it thaws.

■ Wind electric heating tape (available at your hardware store) around the pipe in close loops and plug it in.

■ Sweep a propane torch (with flame-spreader attachment) back and forth along the pipe, being careful not to stop moving the torch and not to get the pipe so hot that you can't touch it. Be sure to place a sheet of flame-retardant material against any other surface that may come within the torch's sweep.

True Value Tip

TO KEEP PIPES FROM FREEZING

■ Wrap them in insulation.
■ Turn on a faucet in each line so that it drips, keeping the water moving so it will be less likely to freeze.
■ Set all thermostats to at least 45 degrees Fahrenheit, so that the inside temperature in any room never drops below freezing.
■ Shut off and drain pipes to outside faucets before the first frost.

STEAMING FAUCET

If steam is coming from a closed or partly open hot water faucet, the hot water heater is over-heating, which is a very hazardous situation. The heater could blow up or there could be electrical shorts. Immediately do the following:

1. Turn on *all* hot water faucets in your home.

2. Turn off the power to the hot water tank but leave on the water supply.

3. When cold water begins flowing from the hot water faucets, turn them off.

4. Call a plumber to inspect the hot water tank.

Know-how

NO DRIPS, NO LEAKS, NO ERRORS

The most common problems with faucets are drip, drip, dripping and leaking around the base. Here's how to stop a drip or leak from the two most common types of faucet, the compression faucet and ball faucet. Individual parts in your faucet may vary slightly. Other types, such as the cartridge (or two-level) faucet, are best repaired by following the manufacturer's instructions or calling a plumber.

Leaking around the handle of a compression faucet

The problem is usually in the packing nut.

1. Before working on the faucet, turn off the water supply at the nearest valve and open the faucet to drain the water.

2. If the faucet is a cross-handle model, unscrew the handle and remove it. If it's a column-handle model, pry the cap off with a screwdriver, unscrew the handle, and gently pry the handle from the bottom.

3. With an adjustable wrench, unscrew the packing nut with a counterclockwise motion and pull it out.

4. Remove the packing string and O-ring from the nut and replace them with new packing string and a new O-ring.

5. Reassemble the faucet and check to make sure the leak has stopped.

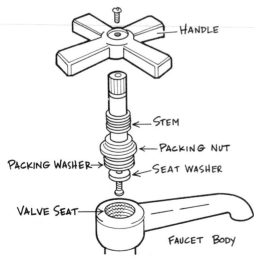

Dripping compression faucet

The cause is usually the washer or the valve seat.

1. Pull out the packing nut by following steps 1, 2, and 3 above.

2. Remove the brass screw at the bottom of the packing nut that holds the seat washer in place. If the washer looks worn, replace it with a same-size washer. Also see whether the valve seat is pitted, corroded, or worn. If it looks okay, reassemble the faucet and test to see if the leak has stopped.

3. If it's still leaking, remove the packing nut again so that you have access to the valve seat. If the valve seat isn't built into the faucet, unscrew it with an Allen wrench, turning counterclockwise. Then remove it and replace it with a new valve seat. If the valve seat can't be unscrewed, use a seat grinder to restore the seat's facings. Screw the seat grinder into the seat to secure a good fit. Then turn it back and forth several times to regrind the facings. Reassemble the faucet to see if the leak has stopped.

Leaking around the handle of a ball faucet

1. Before working on the faucet, turn off the water supply at the nearest valve and drain out the remaining water.

2. Tighten the cap by turning it gently clockwise at the grooved edge with the cap wrench in the manufacturer's repair kit. If you don't have such a wrench, use a pair of slip-bolt pliers or a plumber's wrench covered with a soft cloth to avoid damage.

Dripping ball faucet

1. Turn off the water supply at the nearest valve and drain out the remaining water.

2. Remove the handle by unscrewing the set screw with the designated tool in the manufacturer's repair kit

or an Allen wrench, then pull it off. Remove the cap by turning the grooved portion counter-clockwise with the cap wrench in the kit.

3. Pull out the cam, seal, and ball. Then, using needle-nose pliers, remove and replace the two inlet seals and springs.

4. Check the O-rings and replace them if they are worn (they definitely should be replaced if the faucet leaks at the base).

5. Reassemble the faucet by aligning the ball's slot with the pin and the lug with the corresponding notch in the faucet.

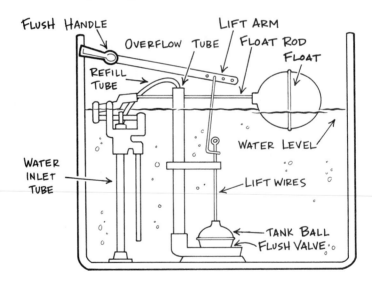

DOUBLE DOUBLE TOILET TROUBLE

A toilet's workings are pretty simple. The flush handle is connected to the lift arm, which raises the tank ball from the valve seat. This opens the discharge pipe so water can flow into the bowl.

When the tank is almost empty, the tank ball falls back onto the valve seat and stops the flow, and water starts refilling the tank. When the float ball on top of the water reaches a preset level, the water shuts off. Simple, but there are lots of things that can go wrong. Here's how to troubleshoot your toilet.

True Value Tip

TESTING FOR A SLOW LEAK

Your toilet can have a slow leak that doesn't make any noise but still wastes hundred of gallons of water a year and makes your toilet work less effectively. To test for this, put ten or so drops of food coloring in your tank. Let stand for a half hour, then check to see if any of the coloring has leaked into the bowl. If so, there is probably a leak. To make sure, mark the water level in the tank with a crayon or thick pencil, turn off the incoming water valve, and let it stand another half hour. If the water level in the tank has dropped below the mark, you definitely have a leak. The probable cause is a worn tank ball or a cracked seal.

STOP THE BANGING

If you hear a bang (or "water hammer") whenever you turn off a faucet, air is trapped somewhere in your system, despite the special chambers that are supposed to prevent this problem. To release the air, try the following: Turn off the main water supply, then open the highest and lowest faucets in the system. When they've stopped dripping, close the faucets and turn on the main water supply. Your pipes will most likely be de-banged!

Water keeps running into the tank

Jiggling the handle may override the problem for a particular flush cycle, but it won't solve the problem.

■ First, flush the toilet and see if the tank ball is dropping firmly into the valve seat. If not, clean the tank ball and valve seat of dirt, rust, or other deposits. Drain the tank by turning off

the shutoff valve and then flushing the toilet. Rub the tank ball and valve seat with steel wool or sandpaper.

■ Another possible cause is improperly aligned lift wires. Bend or straighten so that they're vertical and move smoothly through the guide arm.

■ Sometimes a toilet leaks because the chain keeps getting caught under the flapper valve ball, an element that replaces the tank ball in some newer systems. You can fix this by supporting the chain with a plastic straw. Simply cut it to size and slip it over the chain. Once in place, it will prevent the chain from falling.

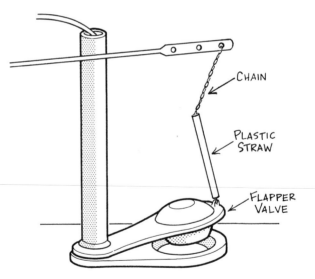

CHAIN

PLASTIC STRAW

FLAPPER VALVE

Water keeps running into the bowl or overflow tube

Lift the float to find out if that stops the problem. If it does, bend the float rod down a little so that the float shuts off the water flow sooner. If it doesn't, you may need to replace all or part of the flushing mechanism (the ball cock assembly), and maybe the overflow tube, too. Signs of corrosion or wear on these parts can be hard to see. If you suspect they're the source of the problem, contact a plumber or, if you feel confident about doing plumbing repairs on your own, replace the parts yourself following the manufacturer's directions.

Weak or no flush

■ Usually the water isn't rising high enough in the tank. Raise the float by bending the float arm or shortening the lift wires.

■ If the toilet isn't flushing at all, or won't flush unless you keep holding down the handle, first see if the handle is loose. If not, make sure the bowl refill tube allows water to drain into the overflow tube. If necessary, bend the bowl refill tube so that it does.

■ If you have well water and a cold climate, occasional weak flushing may occur whenever the ground outside is frozen. Often this problem clears up after several flushes in a short time. Otherwise, it may persist until the ground thaws.

Water dripping from the outside of the toilet

Toilets can start to "sweat" when the water inside the tank is cold and the air outside the tank is warm. The outside air condenses on the cold surface of the tank or bowl and can even drip onto the floor. There are several ways to reduce or stop this problem:

■ Cover the outside of the tank with one of those fitted, terry-cloth covers usually sold as part of a bathroom set.

True Value Tip

EXPERT CAULKING

■ An old playing card makes a great tool for smoothing caulk around tubs, sinks, and shower doors. Pismo Bob Pringle, owner of the True Value hardware store in Pismo Beach, California, points out that the card is stiff enough for the job and that it can be curled or bent into a concave or convex shape. After smoothing out the caulk, use a soft cloth moistened with distilled vinegar to wipe off the excess.

■ Many people find that the caulk around their sinks and tubs keeps cracking and falling out. The reason: Water is heavy. When the tub or sink fills up, the weight of the water widens the seam and puts stress on the caulk. Next time you caulk, fill the sink or tub with water first. Wait a few minutes before starting. Keep it filled as you caulk, and don't drain it until after the caulking has dried. The weight of the water will fully open the seam so the caulk will fill it completely.

■ Insulate the inside of the tank with a special lining available at hardware stores.

■ Hang a special catch tray, also available at hardware stores, immediately below the tank.

■ Have a plumber install a valve that will heat the water inside the tank.

Toilet is leaking on the floor

If a leak is more than just condensation, turn the shutoff valve to stop water from entering the toilet. Tighten all the connections along the water-supply line as well as the nuts under the bolt caps on the base of the bowl. If there are any obvious signs of leaking, replace the part or call a plumber to do so. If there are no such signs, turn the shutoff valve back on. If the problem persists, call a plumber to inspect your toilet. You may need a new bowl or tank.

RESTORING A SHOWERHEAD

Over time, dirt, soap, and mineral deposits block off some of the holes in a metal or plastic showerhead, cutting down the water flow. It's time for the showerhead to take a bath.

1. Unscrew the head. Be careful not to use too much force or you may harm the head or the shower arm. You may need two wrenches: one to hold the arm in place and the other to turn the head. Before using any wrench, cover the surface it's going to grip with two or three layers of masking tape.

True Value Tip

HEAD LOCK
If you have trouble getting a shower head loose so you can clean or replace it, squirt several drops of penetrating oil into or just above the threads and let it set for a day.

2. Wash the head in hot, soapy water, and rinse it with a strong jet of water. This will remove loose deposits.

3. In a small pan, make a cleaning solution of half water and half vinegar at least 2 inches deep. Bring it to a light boil. Put in the shower head so that the holes are immersed in the solution. Let the head simmer in the solution for 5 minutes.

4. Remove the head from the solution and let it sit until it's cool enough to handle. Then brush the holes thoroughly with a bottlebrush or another plastic brush to remove stubborn deposits. Get rid of any remaining blockages by poking through them with a needle.

5. Wrap the threads in one layer of plumber's tape (or, less effectively, coat with petroleum jelly) and replace the head. As before, this may require using two wrenches.

HELP YOUR WATER HEATER LIVE LONGER

You can prolong the life of a water heater and make it more efficient, too, by draining off some of the water every 6 months. This will remove any sediment, rust, or mineral deposits that have accumulated at the bottom. It's easy.

1. Turn off the water supply to the heater (or, if the heater doesn't have a shutoff valve of its own, the water supply to the house).

2. If the heater is electric, turn off the power supply.

3. Open all the hot water faucets in the house so you don't trap air in the pipes.

4. Place a bucket under the drain tap, open the drain, and drain off 3 or 4 quarts of water. If you can't fit a bucket under the drain, run a short piece of flexible hose between the drain and the bucket.

5. Close the drain, turn on the water and power supply, and close all hot water faucets after they've begun to run.

PLUMBING THE DEPTHS OF YOUR SEPTIC TANK

Your septic tank is one thing you'd rather ignore. Most of the time you can, but if you let too many months or years go by, you may pay a dastardly price. Here are guidelines for keeping your septic tank in good working order:

■ Once a year, check the level of sludge in your septic tank. Open the access lid and immerse a long, straight stick perpendicularly into the tank. The stick has to be as long as the tank is deep plus a few feet extra so you can hold it easily. Mark it with feet and inches, starting at the end that will rest on the bottom. Once the stick is inserted into the tank, the sludge will stain the bottom part of the stick and the liquid above the sludge will wet a certain portion of

True Value Tip

DON'T GET YOURSELF IN HOT WATER
Set the temperature on your water heater to 120 degrees Fahrenheit (or "low" or "warm"). This is as hot as you'll ever need tap water to be. This setting will protect your family from accidental scalding. You'll save money on your utility bill, too.

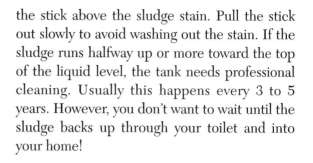

the stick above the sludge stain. Pull the stick out slowly to avoid washing out the stain. If the sludge runs halfway up or more toward the top of the liquid level, the tank needs professional cleaning. Usually this happens every 3 to 5 years. However, you don't want to wait until the sludge backs up through your toilet and into your home!

■ Every month or so, use a commercial septic cleaner (usually administered through the toilet closest to the septic tank) to help break up septic matter.

■ Avoid pouring or flushing chemical products (such as drain cleaners or high-foaming detergents) into the plumbing system. Also, avoid flushing anything more substantial than toilet tissue.

⑦ Down to the Wire
Your Electrical System

A home electrical system doesn't deserve its shocking reputation. You can easily and safely do each of the basic procedures in this chapter. For more involved wiring, call a licensed electrician, unless you're well-grounded in things electric. Even then, check with your local building department to make sure you are allowed to do your own wiring. Some communities allow only licensed electricians to install wiring. Proper compliance with the electrical code ensures that any known dangers can be prevented.

BASIC ELECTRICAL TOOLS

True Value Tip

Here's the gear you need to perform most common electrical maintenance and repair tasks. Two tools from your basic toolbox (*see* Chapter 1) are used to cut wires: slip-joint pliers and a utility knife. The following are specialty tools for electrical work:

■ You will need a **neon tester** to test for power in switches, sockets, and receptacles when the current is on and a **continuity tester** to test for power capability when the current is off.

■ Get a **wire cutter/stripper** to cut small-gauge wires and remove rubber or plastic casing from wires.

■ Buy a pair of **long-nose pliers** to crimp bends and loops in wires and a pair of **lineman's pliers** to twist wires together.

■ Buy a box or bag of assorted **wire nuts** in different sizes.

■ A roll of plastic **electrical tape** will be needed to cover bare wires.

Emergencies

DISCONNECTING THE MAIN POWER SUPPLY

Your home's service panel, the box controlling the electrical circuits that enter your home, probably has a main disconnect: a mechanism that allows you to shut off *all* electric power instantly. Disconnecting the power main is an important first action in an electrical emergency—or threat of an emergency—such as a **fire** (*in an electrical circuit or anywhere else*), **flood, tornado, hurricane,** or **earthquake.** It's also a good idea to shut off all power when doing **electrical work that involves several circuits**, or ones you can't identify.

Here are the different types of main disconnects and how to operate them:

■ **Outer lever:** A lever connecting with two main interior fuses is mounted onto the outside of the box. Shifting the lever to OFF disconnects all the circuits.

■ **Main switch:** Inside the box is a main circuit breaker. Switching it to OFF shuts off all power.

■ **Pull block(s):** One or two main pull blocks are mounted inside the box. Pull to cut the power supply.

■ Some circuit-breaker boxes have **no main disconnect**. Instead, turn every switch to OFF in order to shut off all the power.

SMOKE, SPARKS, OR FLAMES FROM AN APPLIANCE OR PLUG

Appliance is smoking or sparking
1. Don't touch it. Instead, turn it off by flicking a wall switch, pulling out the plug, or disconnecting the main power supply (*see* above).

2. Wait for the appliance to cool, then have it repaired by a professional.

Plug is smoking or sparking

1. Turn off the object by flicking a wall switch or by disconnecting the main power supply (*see* previous page).

2. Wait for the plug to cool, then inspect it for damage. If it needs to be replaced, *see* Plugging Away below.

3. Next test all the outlets in the receptacle where the plug was inserted. Check the fuse or circuit breaker to see if the circuit is still functioning. If not, restore power to the circuit. Then, using a circuit tester, test the outlets. If the receptacle needs to be replaced, *see* Ins and Outs of Outlets below.

Appliance or plug is on fire

1. Get everyone out of the house immediately. Electrical fires can spread very swiftly.

2. Call the fire department.

3. If the fire is still very limited, disconnect the main power supply (*see* above).

4. If the fire is small and you feel competent and safe, attempt to put it out.

Know-how

WORKING SAFELY WITH ELECTRICITY

Your circuit breaker or fuse box

■ Before you work on an electrical circuit, shut off the power to your circuit breaker or fuse box. If you aren't sure which one to turn off, disconnect the main power supply.

■ Record on your fuse or circuit-breaker box which circuits serve which outlets. Be specific and complete. A circuit can cover more than one room, just a single appliance, or certain outlets or overhead lights in several different areas of the house. Also, on the back of each outlet cover, write the number of the circuit serving it.

■ Put a rubber mat directly below the circuit box and always stand on it when you're working there.

■ Never replace a burnt-out fuse with a fuse that has a higher amperage.

Grounding

■ When working with electricity, wear shoes with rubber soles to ground yourself, just in case the power is accidentally restored.

■ If you're working in an area that's flooded or very wet, wear rubber boots and stand above water level on a nonmetal surface *before* shutting off the circuit and *while* working on it.

■ Do not stand on a metal ladder, chair, or table while doing electrical work.

■ Avoid contact with plumbing pipes while doing electrical work; they often serve as a ground for household electrical systems.

Outlets
■ Do not overload receptacles. Put only one plug-in device with multiple outlets into each receptacle. Plug an extension cord directly into one of the receptacle outlets, not into a plug-in device with multiple outlets.

■ Plug in only one extension cord per receptacle and do not create chains of more than two extension cords.

■ When using a three-prong adapter in a two-prong receptacle outlet, be sure to ground the adapter to the screw in the cover plate.

Appliances
■ Always unplug any electrical device before working on it.

■ Never remove a plug by pulling on the cord.

■ Never run cords under a rug, and never place furniture or objects on top of a cord.

■ Keep electrical appliances such as radios, hair dryers, and razors well away from bathtubs and showers. If they're plugged in, they're "live" even if they're not turned on.

Electric shock

Electric shock can interfere with the victim's breathing and heartbeat. Here's how to help someone who has been shocked:

1. Make sure the person has broken contact with the current. If not (often the person can't break away), use a poor conductor of electricity (for example, a rolled-up cloth or plastic sheet or a wooden prod, such as a board or a broom) to break the person free. You could shove away the person yourself, but be careful not to make physical contact for longer than a second or you, too, may be shocked. If there's anyone else around, call out for them to call 911.

2. If the person is not breathing, administer rescue breathing. If there is no pulse, begin CPR. Both procedures are best learned in a class, such as those taught by Red Cross instructors.

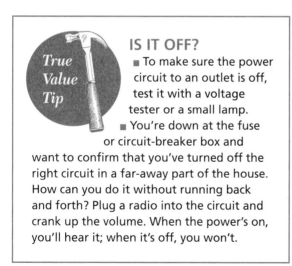

True Value Tip

IS IT OFF?

- To make sure the power circuit to an outlet is off, test it with a voltage tester or a small lamp.
- You're down at the fuse or circuit-breaker box and want to confirm that you've turned off the right circuit in a far-away part of the house. How can you do it without running back and forth? Plug a radio into the circuit and crank up the volume. When the power's on, you'll hear it; when it's off, you won't.

WHAT'S CAUSING POWER FAILURE?

If you repeatedly blow a certain fuse or trip a certain breaker, you need to pinpoint the cause:

■ Unplug and switch off everything on that circuit. Install a new fuse or reset the breaker. If the problem still exists, consult an electrician.

■ If the problem seems to be gone when everything is disconnected, turn on one plug or switch at a time to see if the circuit is being overloaded. If it is, you will reach a limit where the fuse blows or the circuit breaks. You now have three alternatives: take some appliances, lights, or electrical devices off the circuit; be careful not to use too much electricity on that circuit at any one time; or have your circuit(s) rewired to prevent overloading. If you have a fuse box, do not simply replace the old fuse with a higher-amperage fuse. This is not safe.

■ Another possibility is that the problem is consistently caused by a specific defective appliance, electrical device, outlet, or switch. Connecting power to each of these individually, with everything else unconnected, should identify the culprit if there is one. If you suspect a certain appliance or device, try plugging it into different outlets to see if you get the same results. Once you've found the problem, you can decide whether you want to deal with it yourself or turn it over to a professional.

■ If none of the above three strategies helps you to figure out the problem, there is probably a short somewhere in your house's wiring. Consult an electrician right away.

PLUGGING AWAY

You can prevent bigger electrical problems by taking bad plugs off and putting good ones on. It's time to replace a plug as soon as possible when the plug is cracked or broken, the prongs are loose, or there's a dark spot anywhere on the plug (a sign of a possible short). If the cord has worn out, the plug's just as old, so replace it, too. A bad plug can be the reason an appliance isn't working, but check other appliance parts and the receptacle before changing the plug.

There are two types of plugs. A round-wire plug can have either a flat or round casing; it's used on vacuums, irons, and other high-amperage appliances. If there is a third prong, it's a grounded plug. A flat-wire plug (also known as a zip-cord plug) always has a flat casing; it's found on lamps, clocks, radios, and other low-amperage appliances.

GROUND

Replacing a round-wire plug

1. Cut the old plug from the cord squarely at the plug's base.

2. Gently pry off the new plug's outer cover (surrounding the prongs) with a screwdriver.

3. Insert the end of the cord into the base of the new plug. Tie an Underwriter's knot in the wires. If there are three wires (the third is a ground), pull the knot down snugly into the plug before going on.

4. Strip ½ inch of insulation from all of the cord's wires. Twist each wire so that the strands are tight and loop it clockwise around the nearest

UNDERWRITER'S KNOT

screw. Tighten the screws, tucking in any loose strands. If there are three wires, the third is the ground; put it under the bottom screw near the round prong.

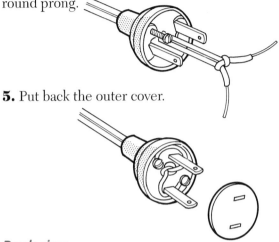

5. Put back the outer cover.

Replacing

1. Cut the old plug from the cord squarely at the plug's base.

2. Insert the end of the cord into the slot at the base of the new plug.

3. Push the lever or the two casing parts to secure the cord in the plug. This forces interior prongs into the cord, completing the circuit.

INSERT THE CORD INTO THE
SLOT AND CLOSE THE LEVER

QUICK
CONNECT
PLUGS

INSERT THE
CORD INTO THE
CORE AND PUSH THE
PRONGS TOGETHER

INS AND OUTS OF OUTLETS

You hunker down in your favorite recliner, pick up your favorite magazine, turn the switch on your reading lamp—and the light doesn't come on. The bulb's okay. Is something wrong with the lamp? Maybe. Before you declare the lamp guilty, try plugging something else into the same receptacle. If it, too, doesn't work, the culprit is probably the receptacle. Follow these guidelines to test and, if necessary, replace it.

First, determine whether the receptacle is receiving current:

■ With the electricity still on, insert a voltage tester's two prongs into the two vertical slots of each outlet. If the tester's light goes on, the current is coming in, and you can proceed with step 1 below.

■ If the tester's light does *not* come on, check the circuit breaker or fuse box. If the fuse for that circuit is blown or the breaker is switched to OFF, restore power to the circuit and test the receptacle again. If the light goes on, go to step 1 below.

■ If the circuit is *not* broken in the circuit breaker or fuse box, check the tester in another receptacle to make sure the tester is working. If the tester and the circuit are apparently working and the voltage tester still doesn't light in the receptacle, call a professional electrician to check for other possible problems in your electrical system.

If the power is reaching the receptacle, replacing it will solve the problem. Follow these steps:

1. Turn off the power to that circuit at the circuit breaker or fuse box. Test the receptacle with the voltage tester to make sure the power is off.

True Value Tip

WHERE'S THAT WIRE SUPPOSED TO GO?

Instead of making a drawing of the locations of the wires before you replace a receptacle, you can label each wire with a small piece of masking tape that indicates exactly where that wire connects to the receptacle. For example, you might stick a piece of tape onto a wire and write "silver"to remind you that it goes under the silver screw.

2. Unscrew and remove the cover plate. Unscrew the top and bottom screws holding the receptacle in the box and pull out the receptacle as far as the wires will allow.

3. Before disconnecting wires from the old receptacle, sketch a diagram showing where each wire is connected to the receptacle so that you can follow the diagram to repeat the same connection pattern in the new receptacle. Creating a clear, accurate diagram will help ensure that the proper connections are made, which on most receptacles means:

■ black or red wires ("hot") to brass screws on the upper side of the receptacle (usually the left side)

■ white wires ("neutral") to silver screws on the opposite upper side

■ green or bare copper wire ("ground") to the green or dark screw near the bottom of the receptacle

4. Disconnect the wires from the old receptacle and, following your diagram, connect the wires to the proper terminals on the new receptacle. Making the new connections may involve re-bending the ends of a wire so it fits around the screw.

5. Restore power to the circuit and test both outlets of the receptacle with a voltage meter to make sure they work. Put back the cover plate.

True Value Tip

THE RIGHT RECEPTACLES FOR WET AREAS

In bathrooms, kitchens, and areas exposed to the weather, the moisture increases the risk of shock from electrical receptacles. In these locales, replace standard receptacles with ground-fault interruptor (GFI) receptacles. They immediately detect hazardous leaking of electricity and shut off the power. A built-in reset button allows you to restore the power safely. These receptacles are required by building codes in most areas for new construction.

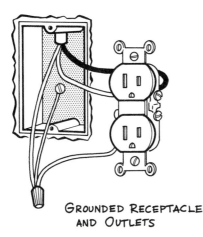

GROUNDED RECEPTACLE
AND OUTLETS

SWITCHING A SWITCH

Sometimes the flick of a wall switch doesn't work. You're still in the dark. First check possibilities other than the switch. Is the power off in that circuit? Is the lamp unplugged? Bulb blown? If everything else is in good shape, you need a new wall switch. The following procedure works for the most common kind of switch: housed in a metal box, with two brass-colored terminals. For other switches, consult a professional electrician.

1. Turn off the circuit at the circuit breaker or fuse box.

2. Unscrew the cover plate, then unscrew the top and bottom screws that attach the switch to its box.

3. Pull out the switch as far as the wires will allow. Without touching any of the wires, note how they are connected to the switch. In most cases, the switch is connected to two black ("hot") wires. These are the only wires that will need reconnecting. Behind most switches run two other, unconnected wires: a white ("neutral") wire and a green ("ground") wire. These wires can be left in place.

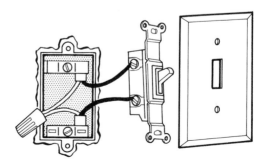

4. Test the switch with a voltage tester to make sure the power is off. Place one of the tester's prongs against the metal box and touch the other prong, in turn, to each brass terminal screw (where the black wires are connected). The tester's light should not shine at either touch. If it does, the power is still on; recheck the service panel to make sure you've cut off the right circuit.

5. Disconnect the two black wires from the old switch and connect them to the same terminals on the new switch. The new switch may not have exactly the same kind of terminals, but they'll be in the same relative position (one above the other). You may have to bend the wires so they fit around the right screws.

6. Reconnect the switch to its box, restore the power, put the cover plate back on, and flip the new switch on.

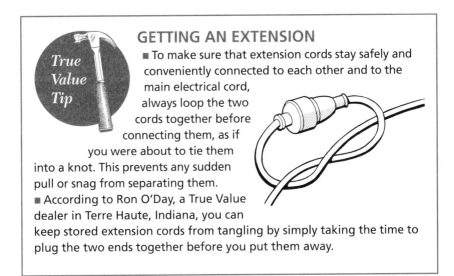

True Value Tip

GETTING AN EXTENSION

■ To make sure that extension cords stay safely and conveniently connected to each other and to the main electrical cord, always loop the two cords together before connecting them, as if you were about to tie them into a knot. This prevents any sudden pull or snag from separating them.

■ According to Ron O'Day, a True Value dealer in Terre Haute, Indiana, you can keep stored extension cords from tangling by simply taking the time to plug the two ends together before you put them away.

BRIGHT IDEAS

True Value Tip

■ An illuminated lever allows you—or a guest—to find a light switch instantly, even if the room is completely dark. Quick illumination can provide safety as well as convenience. Consider installing lighted wall switches in your basement, attic, entry, and bathrooms.

■ You don't have to fumble around in a dark room after you've switched off the light. A time-delay switch—as easy to install as a regular switch—will give you an extra 30, 45, or 60 seconds of light, for safety's sake.

■ A flickering electric bulb may still have a lot of life in it. It may just be dirty. Try cleaning it by rubbing the base of the bulb with a pencil eraser, then giving it a few light strokes with a metal file.

■ Removing a broken bulb from its socket can be difficult and dangerous if you try to do it with your fingers or with a conventional tool. Instead, use a raw potato to twist it out! Just whittle the potato to size, jam it into the broken base, and slowly turn it counterclockwise. If you don't have a potato, try a bar of soap or a cork.

⑧ Keeping Warm and Staying Cool

Your Heating and Air-conditioning Systems

The worst time to find out your furnace isn't working is the first night the temperature drops outside. It's almost as bad when your air-conditioning breaks down on the hottest, most humid day of the year. You can ensure your comfort all year long by doing a bit of maintenance and checking the systems each year before you need them.

Which jobs can you do yourself, and which are for the pros only? In most cases, routine maintenance of a heating system usually requires only a good scout's knowledge of the manuals relating to your particular system and a watchful eye. However, it's generally advisable to let professionals handle big repairs as well as inspect and service your system annually—which, in most climates, is best done during the summer. Call your gas company immediately if any problems develop with a gas furnace—gas is volatile, and gas systems are more complicated than other kinds.

Many furnace installers sell service plans, whether or not they originally installed your system. Many utility companies offer a range of service plan options for gas-fired systems.

Emergencies

NO HEAT

First, check the following, in this order:

■ Is there a general power failure? Find out by turning on lights on various circuits.

■ Is the thermostat down or off? If so, adjust it.

■ Is the system's emergency switch on? If not, turn it on.

■ Is the system getting electrical power? If a fuse is burnt out, replace it; if a breaker is tripped, reset it.

■ If there is a pilot light, make sure it's lit.

If you still can't get the heat working, try the following:

Oil-burning system

1. Check the oil supply level with a long stick marked off in feet and inches. Dip it perpendicularly into the oil tank until it strikes bottom. Remove the stick and check how high the stick is coated. If the tank is very low or empty, have it filled.

2. If there's plenty of oil, press the system's safety relay button one time.

3. If heat isn't restored, press the burner motor reset button one time.

4. If that doesn't work, call a professional.

Warm-air system (oil- or gas-burning)

1. Turn off the power to the furnace. There may be a button on your furnace, or you may have to turn off power at the circuit breaker or fuse box.

2. Inspect the furnace motor's fan belt. If broken, replace; if slipped, reset. (*See* the fan belt section of Warm-air system Know-how below.)

Hot-water system

Try releasing trapped air from each radiator. (*See* How-water system Know-how below.)

Steam-heat system

Check the water gauge and, if necessary, allow more water into the system until the proper level is reached. (*See* Steam-heat system Know-how below.)

LEAKING GAS

Whenever you smell gas in the house:

1. Call for everyone to leave the house immediately because of the high risk of explosion or fire.

2. Do not turn on any electricity or light a match. Instead, do the following in order:

■ Extinguish all open flames and sources of strong heat, such as electric stove burners or space heaters.

■ Turn off all gas appliances, including all burners on a gas stove.

■ Shut off the main gas supply valve at the meter.

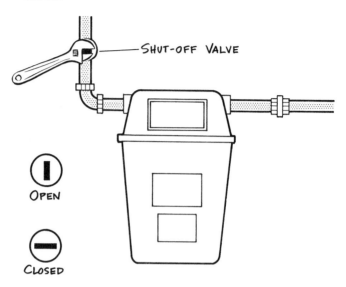

SHUT-OFF VALVE

OPEN

CLOSED

3. Open all windows in rooms that smell of gas and then get out of the house yourself.

4. From the nearest telephone, call your utility company to send a representative. Do not turn on the main gas supply valve or go back in the house until the representative says it's okay.

Know-how

BE A HOT SHOT

Here's how to maintain a warm-air, hot-water, or steam-heat system.

Warm-air system

In most warm-air systems, the air is heated by an oil- or gas-fired furnace. A blower or fan then moves the warm air through ducts, baseboards, or registers into the home.

■ **Clean or replace the filter every month.** A clogged filter reduces air flow and taxes the furnace's motor. Turn off the furnace before cleaning or replacing the filter.

■ **Clean the blower or fan once a year.** First, turn off the furnace completely. Then open the blower or fan compartment. In most **gas-fired systems**, the blower compartment can be accessed by removing the nearest furnace panel or by opening a special access door. In most **oil-fired systems**, the fan compartment can be accessed by unbolting the transformer and moving it aside. Clean the exposed blower or fan blades with a bottlebrush and, if possible, vacuum to remove debris.

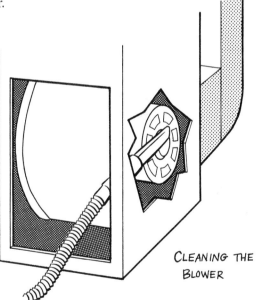

CLEANING THE BLOWER

■ **Lubricate the motor once a year (unless the manual says it's self-lubricating).** Locate the oil ports at one or both ends of the motor. Squirt each cup with 4 to 6 drops of SAE 10W30 oil (available at hardware stores).

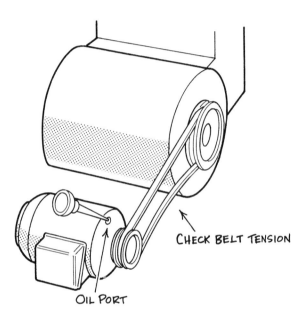

CHECK BELT TENSION

OIL PORT

■ **Inspect the fan belt once a year.** If the motor has a fan belt, inspect it once a year (you can do it at the same time you lubricate the motor). If the belt is worn, replace it. If it gives more or less than ⅓ inch when pressed, tighten or loosen the bolt.

■ **Inspect visible ducts every few months.** To repair a loose duct, first clean all edges, using a nonflammable fluid. Dry thoroughly. Reattach the duct tightly with sheet metal screws and then cover all seams with pressure-sensitive, aluminized tape, pressing out any air bubbles in the tape.

True Value Tip

UPGRADE PILOT LIGHTS

Older gas furnaces, stoves, and water heaters have pilot lights that not only use up fuel need-lessly but can be a safety hazard (gas fumes will go into the air should the light accidentally go out). Replace any pilot light you have with a safer, more economical electric ignition unit. Call your utility company for information.

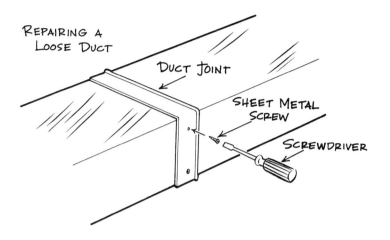

REPAIRING A LOOSE DUCT

DUCT JOINT

SHEET METAL SCREW

SCREWDRIVER

■ **Insulate ducts in unheated areas of the house.** All the ductwork in your basement, attic, or crawl space should be covered with 2 inches of fiberglass insulation to avoid leaks and undue influence of outside air temperature. To insulate a duct, wrap it securely in a batt of spiral R-8 or R-11 insulation. Then seal each joint between batts with aluminized tape.

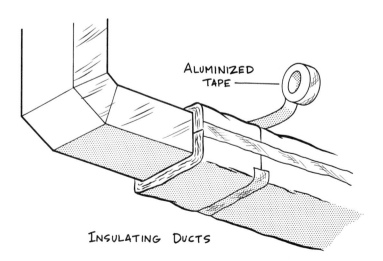

ALUMINIZED TAPE

INSULATING DUCTS

Hot-water system

Hot-water systems heat water in a boiler (gas, oil, or electric), then pump it through pipes to convectors or radiators.

■ **Lubricate the pump and motor.** Unless the manual says the pump and motor in your system are self-lubricating, oil them in the fall and spring, just before and after maximum use. First, shut off the power and wait until the aquastat says the system is cool. Then squirt the proper oil in the pump's and motor's oil cup(s) as directed in the manufacturer's guide.

■ **Release trapped air.** Air sometimes gets trapped in convectors and radiators if the system hasn't been used in a while or just after it's been refilled. When this happens, they don't produce as much heat and feel cooler toward the top. If you suspect that air is trapped in a particular convector or radiator, check all others to see if air is also trapped in them. To release the trapped air in a convector or radiator, open the air vent with a screwdriver or radiator key. If air is trapped in more than one convector or radiator, start with the one closest to the boiler.

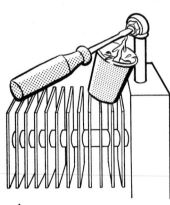

VENTING A RADIATOR

First, hold a cup under the vent at a 45-degree angle. Open the vent and keep it open until water spurts into the cup, then close the vent. Be careful—the water will be hot.

■ **Insulate exposed pipes.** Cover the pipe with pre-formed insulation, held tightly in place by aluminized tape, or wrap it tightly with aluminum tape, overlapping each turn by about ½ inch.

Steam-heat system

In a steam-heat system, a boiler heats water until it steams. The steam travels through pipes to radiators or convectors, where it gradually cools and condenses, sending water back to the boiler.

■ **Inspect the water level.** Every two or three weeks during the cold season, check the water-level gauge to make sure the proper amount of water is in the system. The right level, marked on the gauge, will be at least halfway up. If the water level is lower, turn on the water-supply valve until it rises to the proper level.

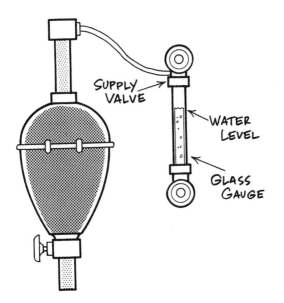

■ **Drain the low-water valve.** Every month during heavy use, turn down the thermostat, put a bucket under the pipe below the low-water valve, and open the valve to let all the sediment deposits drain out. As soon as the water runs clear, close the valve. Water coming out of the pipe will be hot!

DRAIN VALVE

■ **Stop and prevent knocking.** If a one-pipe radiator is making a knocking sound, water at the bottom of the radiator is trapping the incoming steam. To stop the knocking, open the radiator valve all the way and raise the end of the radiator opposite the pipe just a bit higher. Some radiators have bolts in the legs that you can turn with an adjustable wrench to raise the height. For other radiators, insert shims under the legs to hold them up.

MORE RADIANT RADIATORS

True Value Tip

■ Because dark colors radiate heat better than light colors, and a flat finish better than a glossy one, flat black is the best color to paint your radiator. It's approximately 10 percent more effective than glossy white.

■ To make your radiators warmer over the winter months—and save yourself about 10 dollars per radiator—tape heavy-gauge aluminum foil, reflective side out, on the wall behind the radiator. If you don't want to put tape on the wall, cut out a sheet of same-size cardboard and tape it to that or buy an inexpensive heat reflector at your hardware store.

True Value Tip

WARMING UP THE WINTER

■ Heating systems and fireplaces make the air very dry in the winter. This is not only bad for your skin, sinuses, and lungs, but it makes the air feel cooler. The easiest solution is a portable humidifier for the rooms you are in most often, including bedrooms. To find out exactly how dry your air is, you can buy a humidity gauge or hygrometer at your hardware store.

■ After taking a bath during the winter, leave the water in the tub until it has completely cooled. The water will add heat and much-needed humidity to the air.

■ If smoke pours from your wood-burning fireplace when you first light it, the fire is having trouble drawing enough air from the room. The problem is probably that your house is too tight against the outside— not enough leaky windows! Open a nearby window just before you light the fire. This creates a stronger flow of air in the room to proceed up the chimney. As soon as the fire gets going, close the window. You can also try preheating the chimney with a hair dryer (a lit newspaper held up into the chimney often doesn't provide enough heat).

IT'S EASY TO KEEP YOUR COOL

It's easier to keep your home cool than it is to rev up the heat. Maintaining an air-conditioning system is simple.

Central air-conditioning system

■ Check and if necessary replace the air conditioner or furnace filter (whichever your system uses) every month during heavy use.

■ Make sure the outside casing (including the condenser fins) is free from debris. Cut back any shrubbery growth that might block the flow of air. However, the unit should be in the shade, so you may want to plant a bush nearby.

■ Consult the manufacturer's instructions for other maintenance guidelines. For other repairs and annual inspection in the spring, call a professional service person.

Room air conditioners

■ Change or clean the filter behind the indoor (or front) grill every 2 weeks.

■ Clean the indoor and outdoor grills by vacuuming or wiping them with a damp rag.

■ If you have a choice, install an air conditioner in a northern or eastern window or wall (northern is better) rather than a southern or western one. Without the summer sun hitting it for so many hours, it won't have to work so hard to produce cool air.

■ If you're installing the air conditioner in a wall, the higher up the wall you can place it, the better, because hot air rises and collects near the ceiling.

True Value Tip

JET STREAM

■ If you live in a house with a stairway to a cellar, basement, or deep crawl space, you can cool down the first and second floors by opening up the cellar door and turning on a floor fan at the top of the stairway. Aim the flow into the house so that cool air from below the ground is drawn inside. Try it first with all windows closed. Then see if you get a better result by slightly opening a basement window (if you have one) and some of the first- or second-floor windows—especially in rooms you use a lot.

■ You can use a similar setup to draw hot air into an attic that has a window (a stairway isn't necessary as long as there's an opening). Install a fan in this window and aim the flow outward so that hot air from inside the house is expelled. Again, try it first with all windows closed, then experiment with opening some of the windows in the rooms that you want to be the coolest.

AIR-CONDITIONING TURN-ON

True Value Tip

Fran Levinsoll of Florida bought an air conditioner at an appliance store, but it wasn't until she overheard her local True Value dealer that she began saving electricity when starting it. The dealer was explaining to someone that it does no good to turn an air conditioner up to its highest setting to cool down a room more quickly. You might as well begin with a low setting and turn it up 20 minutes later if you want a cooler temperature.

CUTTING YOUR HEATING AND COOLING BILLS

■ A setback-style thermostat, available at hardware stores, can reduce your heating bill enough to pay for itself in a year or two. You can set it to turn the heat down a specified amount for a particular length of time, such as when you're asleep or away from the house during the day.

■ Weather-stripping your windows and doors will help prevent los of heat or cool air (*see* Chapter 5).

■ During all seasons of the year, keep fireplace dampers closed when the fireplace isn't in use.

■ In the winter, open the curtains and blinds on the sunny sides of your house during the day so you can benefit from solar heating. At night, cover all windows to keep in heat.

■ In the summer, to wean yourself from too much dependence on air-conditioning, try keeping all windows open during the night so that cooler air can collect inside the house; close the windows during the day so that the cooler air stays in. Cover windows with curtains or blinds during the day, if only partially, to prevent solar heating.

■ During the winter, shut off unused or rarely used rooms.

■ Experiment with the thermostat to see if you can be just as comfortable with a lower temperature setting in winter or a higher setting in summer.

■ The single best thing you can do to minimize costly heating and cooling bills is to get an energy audit of your house. Call your utility company and set one up. Many offer the service for free, others at a nominal cost that is well worth it. You are under no obligation except to yourself.

True Value Tip

SAVING ON THE BOTTOM LINE

Luis Munoz's True Value dealer tipped him off to a costly heat-loss problem in his home. He was told to check for drafts underneath all the baseboards running along outside walls—a common problem in wood frame houses like his. Sure enough, he found a couple; as advised, he removed the baseboards and caulked the underlying cracks at the base of the wall.

⑨ Out and About
Home Exterior

Wind, water, dirt, and critters are trying their best to get inside your home and do their worst. Every now and again, play Spiderman and check out the roof, outside walls, and other exterior features. Finding loose shingles, small cracks, or evidence of insect infestation early can save homeowners a great deal of time and money later on. Pay particular attention to areas where water might collect or seep in. Poor drainage is probably the most frequent source of exterior trouble spots.

Emergency

LEAKY ROOF

Taking along a strong flashlight, locate the source of the leak in the attic, eaves, crawl space, or ceiling directly below the roof. Immediately put a large bucket under it to collect water until the leak can be repaired. If you can see the hole, drive a wire or long nail through it to help you locate it from the outside. If it's a small hole, you may be able to stop the leak temporarily by applying a small wad of caulking compound directly over the wire or nail and smoothing the edges at least an inch around the hole.

Inspect the roof to find the source or cause of the leak. If you've driven a nail or wire through an interior hole, look at that spot and at the surrounding roof, especially uphill, since water often travels downhill from the exterior source of the leak before penetrating inside surfaces.

Tile, slate, or asbestos shingles are difficult to repair. If your roof is covered with any of these materials, call in a roofer. Wood or asphalt shingles are easier to repair, so you may want to try the following repairs yourself; if the roof is still leaking, then call the roofer.

If the shingle is loose but not damaged
1. If you've previously driven a nail or wire through this shingle or another one from inside, remove the nail or wire before repairing and cover any puncture with cement.

2. Glue the tile with roofing cement.

True Value Tip

LIFELINE
Whenever you're working on the roof, make this your first move: Tie one end of a thick rope securely around your waist and the other end securely around the chimney or another strong feature. You'll have something to hold on to if you start to slip or slide. Make sure the rope is just long enough to allow you to move freely while working but not so long that it will allow you to fall beyond reach of the edge of the roof.

3. Nail the tile in place with galvanized roofing nails.

4. Cover the nail heads with cement.

If the shingle is torn or damaged

A wood or slate shingle has to be replaced as soon as possible. You may be able to repair an asphalt shingle temporarily (for a year or more). If the tear is fairly clean, secure the two edges of the tear with a line of galvanized roofing nails and then cover the tear and the nails with roofing cement. If the shingle is badly torn or damaged, cut off the torn or damaged part, then create a patch for this part from another shingle. Glue the patch in place with roofing cement. Then nail the edges and cover both the edges and the nails with roofing cement.

If the roof flashing is loose

Roof flashing are the metal strips that seal vulnerable edges on the roof: where two different houses, eaves, or dormer roofs intersect (called a valley), where a roof meets a chimney, or where a porch or addition roof joins an outside wall.

■ If you suspect the source of the leak is around a certain area of valley flashing, lift up the ends of each shingle that overlaps that area and apply roofing cement underneath to reseal it tightly against the flashing.

■ If you suspect the leak is occurring around chimney flashing, first see if you can pull the vertical pieces away from the horizontal pieces at the base of the chimney. If you can, clean out any loose mortar, push the vertical piece back into the base flashing, and remortar the connection. Then coat all the chimney flashing with roofing cement.

■ If you suspect the leak is happening where a porch or addition roof meets an outside wall, coat the meeting point with roofing cement.

Moisture during a cold winter

There are three possible reasons for moisture below the roof in an attic, eaves, or crawl space during a cold winter:

■ There could be an icy buildup, called an ice dam, on a nearby roof edge or intersection. A dam occurs when water runs down the roof and freezes over a cold area. As the dam grows, water backs up behind it, gets under the shingles, and leaks into the attic or eaves. To locate a dam, look for bulging shingles on roof edges and intersections outside and below the interior patch of wetness. Also check below spots on the roof where snow melts faster than elsewhere. To remove a dam, gently pick away at the ice with a pointed tool, being careful not to hurt the shingles. To keep dams from forming, make sure that your attic and eaves are adequately and uniformly insulated and that all attic ridges and eaves are well ventilated.

■ Your attic insulation could be inadequate or damaged. Consult a hardware store or insulation company to reinsulate for the most appropriate R-value.

■ Your attic could have inadequate ventilation. Consult a hardware or home-care professional about installing more effective insulation vents along the attic or eve ridge.

Know-how

TOP GUNNING

Over time, external building materials swell and shrink, split and splinter, and wear and warp. Sneaky cracks, holes, and gaps form and keep on growing. When you keep watch over your house, look for these breeches of security:

- between the frames of windows or doors and the house

- between pieces of siding and at the corners of the house

- between siding and foundation masonry

- along the underside of eaves next to the house

- around vents, skylights, and plumbing or electrical fixtures

- around chimney caps and flashing

Every year, ideally after the spring rains, inspect all these places for cracks, holes, and gaps. Gently probe existing caulk or mortar with a screwdriver to see if it's loose. Handle any problem spots in the following ways.

Cracks, holes, or gaps in wood, siding, and shingles

Fill them with acrylic latex, vinyl latex, butyl, silicone, or oil-based caulk. Consult with a dealer to determine the most practical caulking to suit your needs. Here's a brief overview:

■ **Acrylic latex** is good, all-around caulking that's easy to apply.

■ **Vinyl latex**, lower in cost than acrylic latex, is less durable.

■ **Butyl** has the versatility of acrylic or vinyl latex and holds paint somewhat better but, because of its consistency, is harder to apply.

■ **Silicone** provides the strongest bond of all, but it's expensive, somewhat difficult to apply, and doesn't hold paint well. (Paintable silicone caulking is available, but the bond isn't as strong.)

■ **Oil-based** is low in cost, easy to apply, and holds paint well but doesn't provide a very strong bond.

Caulking is packaged three ways: a rope coil (applied by hand), bulk caulking in a can or tube (applied with a putty knife), or a disposable cartridge (applied with a caulking gun). The last is the most convenient and popular for big jobs. Consult with a dealer to determine which is best for your needs and follow the application guidelines on the package.

Caulking with a disposable cartridge clipped inside a caulking gun is one of the easiest and most popular ways to go about the task. Just follow these easy steps:

1. Cut open the tip of the cartridge at a 45-degree angle.

2. Puncture the interior seal of the cartridge by poking a nail through the hole you've just cut.

3. Pick up the gun, extend the plunger-style handle all the way out, and place the cartridge in the cradle.

True Value Tip

4. Push the handle back in as far as you can, then turn it so that the end of the handle faces down, which puts the trigger into operation.

5. To apply the caulk, place the nozzle at a 45-degree angle into one end of the crack so that the tip opening is level with the bottom of the crack. Then squeeze the trigger slowly. When the caulk begins emerging from the tip, slowly move the gun forward in the crack, continuing to hold it at a 45-degree angle.

TIP FOR TIPS

You can prevent the tip of a caulking gun from drying out and clogging between uses. Wipe the tip clean, poke it clear with a nail, then cover it with a slip-on pencil eraser or an electrical cap.

Cracks, holes, or gaps in masonry
Fill the problem with mortar.

1. Chisel all loose mortar from and around the area to be filled in.

2. Mix an appropriate-size batch of mortar in a bucket, following the directions on the package.

3. Wet the area to be filled in with a fine hose spray or a spray bottle; keep the area and the mortar wet while you work.

4. Using a trowel, apply mortar to fill in the crack, hole, or gap. Press firmly and allow the mortar to mound slightly above surface level.

5. Scrape away excess mortar and finish the filled area so that it blends into its surroundings.

6. Moisten the filled area with spray when you've finished. If possible keep it moist over the next two days to help ensure good setting.

CRACKING UP

The next time you have a spare hour or two, stroll around outside your home and take a good look at all the concrete sidewalks, driveways, or patios. See any cracks? If you just walk on by, they'll get bigger and tougher to fix. Even if the crack reopens every now and then as the ground settles, it's best to keep it small by repairing it after each reappearance.

1. Wait after a rain until cracked concrete is completely dry. Chisel the sides until they are smooth and the bottom of the crack is slightly wider than the top. Then clean out the crack with a wire brush.

2. Make an appropriate-size batch of mortar in a bucket and mix in epoxy concrete as directed. This mixture typically dries within an hour so time your repair work so that you finish in 30 to 40 minutes. If the work might take longer, divide it into two or more sessions, so that each session lasts considerably less than an hour. If you're filling in a large crack, apply a series of shallow layers or rings, allowing drying time in between each layer or ring.

3. Using a trowel, fill the crack with the mixture, packing it in firmly so that it mounds slightly over the surface. Then smooth it even.

4. When you finish filling the crack, clean all the tools right away with turpentine or paint thinner.

True Value Tip

CONCRETE FACTS

■ Got a crack in a concrete patio, porch, or walkway that you can't repair just yet? To keep it from getting worse—and, left alone, it inevitably will—True Value dealers advise packing it with sand and then sealing it with waterproof tape until you mix the concrete to fill it. If it's winter and the ground is frozen, try getting rid of locked-in moisture before you pack the crack by going back and forth over it with a propane torch.

■ Cement is tough to store. Don't keep large stocks of cement on hand—it can easily be ruined by moisture. Buy just the amount you'll need for each job as it comes. Always keep it in a dry place and raised off the ground. If you have a number of unopened bags, store them close together: lying on top of one another in side-by-side piles. Cover unopened bags with a plastic sheet or tarpaulin. Keep opened bags securely closely and sealed in large plastic bags. If you only have a small amount of cement left, store it in an old coffee can with a plastic cover. If any cement in a bag has formed a lump that won't break when you squeeze it by hand, throw away the entire bag.

■ Cleaning your concrete or asphalt driveway regularly not only makes it look nicer but keeps it in good condition. Here's the quick-and-easy method: Hose the driveway until it's soaking wet, then sprinkle a thin layer of environmentally safe detergent all over it. Use a broom to work the detergent into the surface. Hose the driveway again until clear water runs off it.

GET YOUR MIND IN THE GUTTER

If your gutters leak or aren't hung properly, you'll have drips, splashes, gushes, puddles, and pools on a rainy day. Even worse, the water will damage the house's foundation. Twice a year, fall and spring, do an inspection and cleaning.

1. Clean the gutter of all debris. It's usually safer and easier to work from a ladder rather than the roof. Remove the debris by hand and throw it on the ground or onto a tarp.

2. If there are screens covering the down spouts, make sure they aren't clogged or broken. If any are, clean or replace.

3. Test the gutter hangings for looseness. Nail or screw them in as necessary (in gutters hung with cross-straps, the nails or screws for the straps may be underneath the nearest shingle). If a cross-strap is broken, replace it.

4. Run water into the gutter with a hose or bucket. It should drain right into the down spout. If it doesn't, here's how to fix it: **If water stops or pools anywhere along the gutter except right at the down spout**, reposition the cross-strap's nails or screws until water flows steadily downhill from one end of the gutter to the downs pout. Run water through the gutter again to make sure it works properly. **If water stops or pools at the down spout**, first try clearing it with a strong stream of water. Next, try a plumber's snake (don't use a stick—it could break inside). If the down spout is blocked, clear it of all debris, using the snake followed by a strong hose stream. Then test the gutter again by running water through it.

5. Run water through the gutter again and look for any leaks along the underside. Here's how to repair them: **To repair a small leak (hole less than ½ inch across)**, first mark exactly where it is. Then dry the area and clean away all loose metal, rust, or debris with a wire brush. Using a putty knife, apply a smooth coat of roofing cement to the leaking area. Clean the knife and any spilled cement with turpentine or paint thinner. After the cement has dried (check the label for time), run water through the gutter again to see if the leak has stopped. **To repair a large leak (over ½ inch)**, use a canvas or vinyl patch that's ½ inch larger all the way around than the leak. First, after cleaning the leaking areas (*see* above), apply a smooth coat of roofing cement. Then press in the patch on top of the cement and cover it completely with another smooth layer of roofing cement. Test for leaks after the cement has dried (check the label for time).

True Value Tip

GUTTER TIPS

■ Check the ground immediately below all your gutters for thin spots of grass or depressions in the dirt. These could well be signs of a gutter leaking or overflowing directly overhead. Check the gutter to see if there are leaks.

■ Make sure water leaving each spout drains quickly away from the building. If not, add a spout extension, place a directional device (such as a grooved paver) on the ground immediately below the spout, or dig a 6-inch channel leading at least 3 feet away from the spout and fill it with gravel.

TERMITE PATROL

Like war, termites are hell. Perhaps you've chuckled at commercials that show an entire home collapsing into a pile of sawdust, but if termites colonize *your* home, you won't be laughing. They can rapidly devastate all wooden building materials so keep a sharp lookout for their presence at least once a year, preferably in the spring, their major assault season.

■ Look for "dirt tunnels" on the masonry foundation outside (and inside where possible) and on all pipes that travel through the foundation. Tunnels that run along pipes or across walls look like thin lines of dirt. Tunnel entrances into masonry look like hollow rings of dirt.

■ Peer and probe into all masonry cracks, holes, or crumbly spots for insects or for dirt formations that might be nests.

■ Closely examine all wooden features of the house that are close to the ground, including crawl spaces. Using a small knife or pick, poke into any area that appears rotten or decayed (on painted wood, a peel or blister may lie on top of such a spot). If you can easily penetrate the wood to a depth of ½ inch or more, the wood may have been damaged by termites.

■ Using the same technique, closely examine all other wooden features of the house and yard, including windowsills, door frames, stairs, fences, trellises, and posts.

■ If you find any evidence that there may be termite damage, call an exterminator.

GETTING RID OF A HORNET OR WASP NEST

Sometimes a wasp or hornet nest is easy to spot; you'll see an ingenious papery structure attached to a building or tree. Other times, you have to locate the nest by tracking the movements of residents. If the nest is on or just inside the outside surface of your house, garage, or shed, you'll definitely want to get rid of it for safety's sake. If it's on a tree somewhat distant from your house and out of children's reach, think twice before disturbing it. Aside from conserving nature, you don't want displaced wasps or hornets to move onto or into your house.

■ The most effective way to get rid of a nest is to buy a long-range-shooting chemical spray made for the purpose (available at hardware stores and nurseries). Following the directions on the can very closely, spray after sunset, when the hive is full and the insects are inactive or asleep. Don't remove the nest for a week; wait until there's no activity.

■ A nature-friendly way to destroy a hive is to hit it with a long, hard, well-aimed stream of hose water, making sure to keep spraying the nest until it's a soggy mess. You can also use this method to knock down a nest that you've previously sprayed.

■ Although a counterattack is unlikely with any of these methods, be prepared just in case. Wear protective clothing (all skin covered) and know exactly where you're going to run for cover— preferably inside a nearby door you can shut!

KEEPING OUTDOOR FURNITURE IN GOOD SHAPE

Wooden furniture

■ Mahogany, teak, and other tropical hardwoods are very durable and weather-resistant. It's best to do nothing at all to such furniture except for an occasional cleaning with lukewarm water and wood soap: no sealing, preserving, staining, and definitely no painting. Just let it go gray and age gracefully, even if you have to leave it outside during snowy winters. The beauty of the wood lies in the grain. Any coating would obscure this beauty.

■ If your furniture is made of redwood or cedar, coat it with water sealer every year in the early spring. Special redwood sealer works best on redwood, but other water sealers are okay. Apply sealer indoors (for example, in your garage) or, if outdoors, on a cloudy day or in the shade rather than in direct sunlight. Most people prefer not to paint (with enamel) or stain redwood, since it mars the beauty of the natural wood, but this may be appropriate if you need to cover a discoloration or match pieces to each other. If you do paint or stain, then you don't need to water seal every year. Instead, repaint or restain when worn. Redwood and cedar furniture that's been adequately coated can be left out over the winter, but it's better to put it inside or cover it with a tarp.

■ If your furniture is made of pine, you can water seal the bare wood each year, but it will be better protected from the elements if you paint or stain it. The furniture should also be stored indoors or covered with a tarp during snowy winters.

Metal furniture

■ Aluminum rarely rusts, but it can become discolored, dirty, and pockmarked. To revive it, clean it with detergent-filled steel wool pads followed by a wet cloth rubdown. After it's dry, wax it with the same kind of paste you use on your car. Store it indoors over the winter.

■ Wash wrought-iron furniture in the early spring and late fall with soap and water and apply a coat of wrought-iron wax. Before waxing, touch up any place where the enamel has worn or chipped off. If there's a rusty spot, remove it with steel wool before repainting. If it needs complete repainting and the old coat is in reasonably good condition, first rub it all over with steel wool to provide a biting surface for the new paint. If the old coat is in bad condition, first remove all you can with steel wool, then apply an acid solution that will strip off all remaining paint (ask your dealer what type to buy and how to apply it). Finally, paint it with at least two coats of enamel. Wrought-iron furniture can be left outdoors over snowy winters; but to minimize damage, you may want to keep it indoors.

Plastic, canvas, wicker, or rattan furniture

■ Wash plastic and canvas furniture with soap and water, rinsing thoroughly, at least once a month. If plastic webbing or canvas looks frayed, replace it immediately or put away the piece of furniture until you can, rather than risk someone getting hurt. Store plastic and canvas furniture indoors during snowy winters.

■ Clean wicker and rattan furniture regularly by vacuuming and then washing in mild, soapy water. To preserve it better, give it a thin coat of varnish or enamel paint. You can make some repairs using waterproof glue (consult your dealer) and rustproof tacks. Store it indoors during snowy winters.

OUTDOOR MAINTENANCE TIPS FOR EVERY SEASON

■ When hosing off the outside walls of your house, start at the bottom and work up. Otherwise you create heavy streams of dirt running downward, which can immediately cause stains that require more intensive cleaning. Once you've hosed or sprayed to the top, quickly go back down for a final rinse. If you have wooden clapboard siding, don't direct a hard stream upward on the bottoms of the boards; water can work its way under the boards and behind the siding.

■ Moss often grows on shingles on shady areas of a roof. It usually doesn't cause any problems on asphalt shingles, but it promotes decay of wooden ones, and it doesn't look very good on either kind. You could scrape away the live moss with a square-edged trowel or shovel, but it would take a long time. The job will go faster if you carefully apply a garden fungicide to kill the moss, then come back later to scrape it away; still, you're going to have two lengthy bouts of roof work. George Richtenburger got a tip from his True Value dealer that makes the whole process easier. Throw a powdered, environmentally safe laundry detergent onto the moss from the ground, a ladder, or a nearby window. It kills the moss and will wash away with the next rain. You'll still have to scrape away the dead moss, but it'll be easier than removing live moss.

■ When True Value hardware customers in Pismo Beach, California, have a broken concrete fountain or statue, Pismo Bob Pringle sells them same-color plumbers' epoxy. It adheres to the concrete and can be shaped by sanding or carving.

■ If you water seal your deck every year, the pores of the wood will become clogged. You can wait 2 or 3 years between applications, depending on the product.

■ You can use kerosene to remove roofing tar or cement from tools, but what about your hands or other areas of skin that accidentally get hit? Yes, kerosene will work on them, too, but Caryn Pillowski knows a kinder, gentler substance once recommended by her True Value dealer: vegetable oil, followed by soap and water. She's since found out that margarine and butter also work.

■ Coat your snow shovel with something slick: paraffin, furniture wax, an old candle (just rub it on), or even cooking spray. The shovel will slide in and out of snow much more easily. You can do the same with the chute of your snowblower.

■ It's difficult to keep wooden or concrete steps ice-free during an especially long, heavy bout of winter weather. Wayne Cousins borrowed this trick from his True Value dealer: Cut sections of burlap to exactly fit each step. Place them on the steps, directly over the ice, and slowly pour hot water over them. The water will freeze right away and seal in the burlap, leaving just enough burlap rising above the freeze line to provide good traction for going up and down the steps.

⑩ Going for the Green
Better Lawns and Gardens

Whether your yard is immense or the size of a postage stamp, it's your piece of paradise on earth. It's a place to refresh your senses, play with your family and friends, and admire the beautiful setting you've given your house. For many people, though, the two most feared words in home maintenance are "yard work." Whenever they gaze through their windows and sigh, "Ah, the great outdoors!" they're sorely tempted to add, "Oh, my aching back!" Here are some ways to get more satisfaction out of taking care of your yard. It's all a matter of knowing what's really out there and what it needs to thrive and then putting that knowledge into action. You might still be sore on Monday morning, but you'll be happier about it!

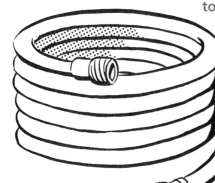

Know-how

CUTTING-EDGE LAWN CARE

It feels good to do a really great job of mowing the lawn. Here are some tips for a season of perfect mowing:

■ Begin mowing in the spring when the grass is about 2 inches high; if you start sooner, you may stunt the new growth. Before the first cutting, make sure the mower blades are clean and sharp. If they're not, use a sharpening stone on them or take them in to a lawn mower dealer or hardware store.

■ Only mow when the grass is dry. Otherwise, you risk clogging the mower with wet grass, missing grass that is plastered to the ground, and pulling out by the roots the grass that sticks to the mower blade.

■ Before every mowing, walk over the entire lawn to remove any rocks, sticks, or debris.

■ For safety, always wear sturdy shoes and ear protectors.

■ When mowing a large lawn area, follow a spiral pattern to minimize unnecessary mower movement between rows and to achieve the most natural look for your lawn. Reverse the spiral the next time you mow the lawn (or for the second mowing in a single session) so that the grass isn't always flattened in the same direction.

■ Mow the lawn whenever the grass gets around 2 inches high. In cooler climates, this will mean more frequent mowing during the spring season of vigorous growth than during the summer season of slower growth. In warmer climates, this will mean more frequent mowing during the summer season.

■ Set the mower blades to cut the grass about 1½ inches high. If you mow grass to less than 1½ inches, you risk not leaving enough blade to absorb the amount of sunlight needed for healthy roots. If the grass is higher than 3 inches, mow twice: first, set higher than 1½ inch; the second set to 1½.

■ Continue mowing into the fall until the grass stops growing (in other words, when mower blades set at 1½ inch stop cutting much grass). You may want to mow across fallen leaves as well as the grass, even if the grass is no longer cutting at a 1½-inch setting, assuming the leaf cover isn't too thick. This provides excellent mulch for the grass during the winter months and helps reduce leaf raking.

FEEDING YOUR LAWN AND PLANTS

Before you can fertilize your lawn, shrubs, and other plants, you have to know what they need to eat. First, identify the different types of grass and plants on your land by taking samples (for grass, small plugs of sod; for plants, pieces of leafy stem and/or photos) to a professional, such as a nursery or gardening center staff member. Second, find out what nutrients your soil requires to support healthy lawn and plant growth. One easy and inexpensive approach is to send a soil sample to your nearest United States

True Value Tip

WHICH WAY DID I MOW?
Here's a suggestion for remembering whether the last mowing was clockwise or counterclockwise: Keep a small rag where you store the mower. When you put the mower away, put the rag *over the handle* if you want to mow *clockwise* the next time. If, instead, you want to mow counterclockwise the next time, don't put the rag over the handle.

True Value Tip

RECYCLE ASHES

Save the ashes from your wood-burning fireplace for your gardens. Once the flowers have bloomed or the vegetables have grown beyond the flowering stage, sprinkle a thin layer over the soil, keeping the ashes from touching the plant stems. The minerals in the ashes are excellent plant nutrients, and many pests (like slugs) hate to move across them.

Department of Agriculture (USDA) office (call for instructions). If you can't interpret the results of the USDA analysis yourself, take them to a professional. A soil sample can also tell you—or a professional—what kinds of grass and plants are most likely to thrive on your land.

A soil test and grass/plant identification will help you determine the best possible fertilizer(s) for your particular needs. In general, however, most lawns and plants benefit from a fertilizer that provides nitrogen, phosphorus, and potassium in a ratio of 3-1-2 (for example, a common package description is 21-7-14). In areas where the soil already contains enough phosphorous, choose a fertilizer without any, since runoff can pollute lakes and streams.

Fertilize only in the spring—beginning after the first time you mow the lawn—and in the first half of summer. In most climates, fertilizing after July can lead to vigorous growth in the fall, which makes grass and plants susceptible to damage during the winter months. Also, guard against overfertilizing, since the chemicals may burn the grass or plants. Follow the instructions on fertilizer packages very carefully. Usually they recommend fertilizing no more than every four weeks.

As a general rule, fertilize after the grass or plants have been watered, because the moisture helps to distribute the fertilizer. It's also wise to avoid fertilizing on days that are windy or likely to be rainy (too much water can wash the fertilizer away).

True Value Tip

RECYCLING A LEAKING HOSE

When an old garden hose has outlived its effectiveness as a watering device, True Value dealers suggest the following uses:

■ Slice a section lengthwise and use it as a blade guard on a hand saw, pruning saw, or ax.

■ Make a temporary patch for a leaking pipe: cut a piece, and hold it on with a clamp.

■ Fit small pieces over the back of a shovel blade or pitchfork head to make safer, more comfortable foot pads.

■ Cut little slits in a length of hose, then wrap the piece around the edges of swings, the metal frames of patio furniture, the bottoms of garage doors, and anywhere else that might benefit from a soft, pliant buffer.

■ Use small, sliced-open sections as hand grips for carrying sheets of metal, glass, or splintery wood or wallboard.

■ Place small, sliced-open sections as protectors under rope or cable that's stretched across something you don't want to mar.

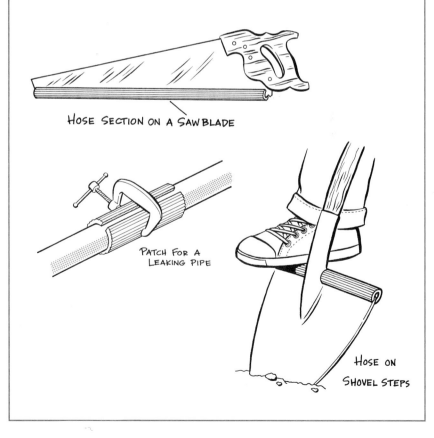

HOSE SECTION ON A SAW BLADE

PATCH FOR A LEAKING PIPE

HOSE ON SHOVEL STEPS

OH, NO, A BALD SPOT

Nothing looks shabbier and reflects more badly on your grass-keeping skills than a lawn with bare spots. You can green those bare spots away with seed or sod. Seeding is easier and more appropriate for small spots. Sodding is more difficult but, if properly done, more likely to yield good, long-lasting results.

■ You can patch a bare spot anytime. If it's late fall or winter (as long as the ground isn't frozen), you can seed the spot in advance for the following spring. In fact, this is the best way to ensure that new grass starts coming up as soon as the next growing season begins. Most of the seed will survive the winter, and you can always add more seed afterward.

■ Before seeding the bare spot, you need to choose the right seed for the site. Most garden supply centers and hardware stores sell grass seed labeled according to the amount of sunlight available (for example, "bright sun," "sun-and-shade," "dense shade"). Usually these mixtures of various types of grass seeds produce grass that blends in well enough with most surrounding lawns. In fact, the new grass may be better suited for the available sunlight than the surrounding grass, as the bare spot itself may indicate.

■ If you want to fill the bare spot with grass that exactly matches the surrounding lawn, take a sample piece of sod to a professional. An alternative is to relocate pieces of sod from somewhere else on your lawn to the bare spot, perhaps by making or expanding a garden or clearing a space for a lawn ornament, paved surface, or plant.

To plant sod in a bare spot

1. If you can, prepare the bare spot before digging out the sod pieces. If the sod pieces are dug out first, keep them moist, but not so wet that they fall apart, and lay them out where they can get sunlight like the rest of the lawn, preferably without blocking other grass. Dig out the entire bare spot to the actual or intended depth of the sod pieces, which, ideally, should be at least 3 inches. Save the dug-out soil for possible use in sodding (*see* step 2). Then puncture the spot randomly with a pitchfork or pointed tool to make the soil more porous.

2. Pack the sod pieces tightly inside the bare spot and tamp them in place with the back of a hoe or your feet. After this tamping, they should be level with each other, forming a slight plateau about ½ inch above the surrounding lawn to allow for settling over the next few weeks. If a piece of sod is too low, bolster it from underneath with some loose soil. It it's too high, dig the hole deeper.

3. Puncture the sod randomly with a pitchfork or pointed tool a few times. Don't damage the sod, but do make sure that it's somewhat porous and that divisions between pieces are broken up a bit.

4. Water the sod well. For the next 10 to 12 days, water the sod enough to keep the soil from drying out. In most cases, this means watering in the early morning and late afternoon on days when there hasn't been enough rain.

True Value Tip

A WICKET'S THE TICKET

Shana Isaly's True Value suggested that she use her croquet wickets to guide her garden hose around flower beds. The guides also prevented sharp turns that cause a kink and block the flow of water.

To seed a bare spot

1. Choose a day that isn't windy. First remove any dead grass, stones, and debris from the spot. Then puncture the spot randomly with a pitchfork or pointed tool so that the soil is fairly loose and full of holes. Level the spot, if necessary, by redistributing loosened soil.

2. Spread the seed as directed on the package. You may want to be a bit more generous in your spreading to ensure good coverage, but don't go overboard. Too much seed can lead to rotting.

3. Water the area slightly so that it's moist without being muddy. Then randomly tamp the area with the back of a hoe or your feet to press more of the seed into the ground.

4. Scatter straw or grass clippings loosely over the area to provide cover for the seed.

5. Using stakes and string (the string running about 1 foot above ground level), mark off the boundaries of the area. Also run some string across the area at various random angles. Tie strips of aluminum foil here and there along the string so that the loose ends can wave in the breeze. This will help keep birds away from the seed.

6. Water the area more thoroughly, but don't let the water form puddles. For the next 2 to 3 weeks, water the area enough to keep the soil from drying out. In most cases, this means watering in the early morning and late afternoon on days when there hasn't been sufficient rain.

AWAY WITH WEEDS

One person's weed is another person's flower. Only you know what things you don't want growing in your lawn. So call *them* weeds and take charge before they do.

If possible, remove individual weeds with a trowel or forked instrument by digging under the roots so that you don't leave any root pieces behind to regenerate. This is most easily done after a big rain when the soil is loose.

If the lawn is overgrown with weeds, a chemical herbicide may be your only choice. Take weed samples to a garden professional. The herbicide should be matched to the specific weed(s) you want to control, and the instructions on the packaging should be carefully followed.

Here's the basic procedure for spraying with an herbicide, whether you use a bottle sprayer or a tank sprayer:

1. Mow and water the lawn 2 to 3 days before the application. This gives the grass time to recover from being mowed and the herbicide time to do its work before the next mowing. Watering plumps up the weeds so they are more vulnerable to the herbicide.

2. Spray individual weeds on a day that's not windy—preferably in the early morning or late afternoon when the sun isn't as hot. Before spraying, make sure that children and pets are kept out of the area and will stay out for several hours until the herbicide has dried. You may even want to post warning signs. While spraying, point the spray nozzle close to the ground and directly at the weed.

3. After spraying, don't water the area for several days or you'll dilute the herbicide. When the weeds have clearly died (it may take a week or more), rake them away to facilitate the growth of new grass.

TAKING TREES AND SHRUBS OFF THE MENU

True Value Tip

Short of surrounding your yard with a high fence buried a foot into the ground, it's tough to completely keep away hungry rabbits and deer. However, you can reduce the damage.

■ Wrap burlap around the bottom 3 feet of all young trees and other trees that show signs of damage. Tie the burlap in place rather than using nails or staples, which can injure the tree.

■ Mulch with shredded pine or sawdust around the base of trees and shrubs, then spray or powder the mulch with an animal repellent. Refresh the repellent at least once a week and after heavy rainfall.

■ On random branches inside the shrubs, hang mesh bags (or pantyhose legs) stuffed with plain bar soap (without scent or lotion) or mothballs.

■ Offer deer a more attractive treat. Place a bale of hay or a salt lick (available at most nurseries) at a secluded edge of your property, a good distance from the trees and shrubs you most want to protect.

GIVING YOUR LAWN SOME AIR

Thatch is warm and charming on top of an English cottage, but it's a cold, strangling monster on top of your lawn. Over time, dead grass, leaf bits, and other debris get locked together on a lawn. If this thatch gets too deep, it starts cutting off air, sun, and water from the living grass.

If you can see a buildup on a small part of your lawn, you can clear it with a hand tool called a thatch rake. If the grass underneath has thinned, reseed by randomly puncturing the ground, spreading seed, and watering well for 2 to 3 weeks.

Thatch does not have to be easily visible on your lawn to be pervasive and damaging. To find out if you have a serious thatch problem, cut pieces of sod 1 inch square and 2 inches deep from several parts of your lawn, keeping track of which piece came from which part. Examine the straw-colored area between the grass and the soil. If it's thicker than ½ inch, you have a thatch problem in that area of the lawn. If most of the pieces are over ½ inch thick, it's probably wise to de-thatch the entire lawn.

1. To de-thatch an entire lawn (or large parts of one), rent a de-thatcher machine. It has rotating spikes that will lift out the thatch without harming much grass. Choose a day that's just after you've mowed, when the grass is shortest. Set the machine to a depth of ½ inch and walk it slowly back and forth over the area in parallel strips, without much overlapping, until you have covered the entire area one time. Rake up the thatch and remove it as you would leaves or grass clippings.

2. Reset the machine to a slightly lesser depth and walk it slowly back and forth over the area in parallel strips, this time perpendicular to the strips you made before. When you've finished, rake up and remove the thatch. Then water the lawn well and, if desired, fertilize it. Although the de-thatcher will have removed a certain amount of grass, seeding or sodding shouldn't be necessary unless it was so before removing the thatch.

BREAKING NEW GROUND

If you're a gardener, you know the special joys of creating a new garden and watching it grow through the seasons. A garden adds new life to your property, your home, your family, and yourself. If you've never been a full-fledged gardener, these tips will help you plan and start a flower or vegetable plot.

Asking first

Before you start digging away, you have to plan your garden carefully. Think about what you want and talk to the pros at a nursery, gardening center, or hardware store.

First, think about where your garden should grow. Draw a sketch, like a floor plan, of your yard, showing all existing and planned features such as gardens, trees, hills, walkways, patios, decks, pools, cooking areas, pet areas, play areas, and buildings (including the house, with windows and outside doors marked). Then indicate each site that might be appropriate for your garden. A good spot:

■ has good sunlight and drainage

■ isn't an obstacle for other activities

■ isn't subject to damage from other activities

■ is relatively easy to reach with a hose and any other cumbersome gardening equipment

■ is easy to protect from predators (for example, by fencing with chicken wire) without disturbing other outdoor functions or causing an eyesore

■ adds to the beauty of the yard, including (possibly) as viewed from inside the house

Once you have a site in mind, you need to pick the plants. Here are the questions to ask:

■ **"How much sunlight do these plants need?"** Before choosing the final site and buying the plants, estimate the hours of direct sunlight on various possible sites during the growing season.

■ **"What are the climate considerations?"** Plants should be selected according to how well they suit the length, the average temperature extremes, and the humidity of the growing season. The plants that will do the best are the ones that are native to your area or that have a history of growing well there. Find out what zone you're in.

■ **"What are the drainage considerations?"**
Some plants tolerate, or even thrive in, areas
with poor drainage. For the good drainage that
most plants need, however, you'll want level
land that isn't near big slopes. Depending on
the situation, drainage can be enhanced by
adding materials to the soil, creating ditches,
raising planting beds, or contouring the area.

■ **"What are the soil considerations?"** The
plants that stand the best chance of thriving are
those that can do well in the existing soil, perhaps with a few additives. Get a professional soil
sample analysis to find out what additives your
soil needs for various plants. In some cases—
especially for certain flower gardens—you may
want to add a layer of topsoil to the plot.

■ **"What are the timing considerations?"**
For example, you many want to plan when different vegetables will ripen so that they all won't
ripen at once, too late in the season, or during an
anticipated vacation. You may want to plan when
different flowers will bloom so that you have
some color throughout the growing season.

■ **"What are the pest considerations?"** You'll
want to know in advance what insects or animals
might show up to harm your plants so that you
can be on the lookout for them and respond
quickly. You'll also want to choose plants that are
not overly susceptible to damage from the insects
and animals that are prevalent in your region.

Breaking ground

Below are the basic steps for starting a garden plot:

1. Carefully mark out the perimeter of the plot with stakes and string. This serves a double purpose. First, you can more easily visualize the future size and shape of your garden and adjust them before you begin digging. Second, the stakes and strings will guide you when you're digging out the plot.

2. Dig up the sod with a shovel to the depth of the blade. If you plan to use the sod as part of the soil, turn it over and break it up well, including the grass. As you're doing this, remove weeds by the roots and throw them into a trash bag or wheelbarrow. If you plan to add a significant amount of topsoil, you may want to preserve pieces of sod to use on bald spots of your lawn. In that case, remove unbroken sod pieces, then break up a few inches of underlying soil. When turning and breaking up the soil, work down one lengthwise strip of the plot at a time, before moving on to the next parallel strip. This will help ensure that you don't miss a spot. After turning and breaking up the soil, go over the whole area again, one strip at a time, and remove any remaining weeds, large rocks, and debris.

3. If you're adding topsoil, do so now, spreading it evenly on top of the existing soil.

True Value Tip

SOIL COLLECTOR

When you're digging a hole in the ground, spread a plastic or cloth sheet next to you and pile the dug-up soil on top. This collector can then be tipped to refill the hole or pulled up to move the dirt somewhere else. Either way, there won't be any extra dirt on the grass.

4. For vegetable gardens and even some flower gardens, it's best to use a rotary tiller to prepare the soil for planting (you can rent one from a nursery or equipment-rental store). If you're *using* a rotary tiller, first remove the stake-and-string barrier around the perimeter of the garden. Then till the plot, working down parallel strips and tilling to the depth of the blade (7 to 10 inches). When you've finished, remove any large stones or debris you've dislodged. Next, spread any soil additives you're using, including fertilizers and compost (up to 3 to 6 inches), evenly across the plot. Till again. If you're *not using* a rotary tiller, spread any soil additives you're using, including fertilizer and compost (up to 3 inches) evenly across the plot. Then, working down parallel strips, shovel the additives into the soil by turning over each spot two to three times.

5. To plant individual seeds or plants, follow the directions that appear on the package or tag—or that the seller gave you—then mark what you've planted with a stake and a water-resistant tag. For rows of the same seed or plant, first mark each row with stakes and string to ensure a straight line, then plant according to directions.

6. When you've finished planting, water the entire plot, stopping well before the water forms puddles.

GARDEN-TOOL WINTERPROOFING

When you're putting away garden tools in the fall, a little care can give them full wintertime protection and a much longer life.

1. After a thorough cleaning with mild soap and water, immediately followed by an equally thorough drying, coat all metal parts lightly with floor wax to prevent rust and corrosion.

2. Rub a small amount of linseed oil into all wooden parts to keep them from drying out and splitting.

3. Store the tools in a dry place away from direct sunlight. Vertical hanging is best so that moisture won't collect. Avoid stacking them or letting them touch the floor.

Putting away your motor

Proper storing of your mower over the long winter months helps improve its performance and extend its life.

1. Drain the gas from the tank.

2. Start the engine again to burn off the few remaining drops in the system.

3. Take out the spark plug, inject a couple squirts of oil into the cylinder, and pull the starter cord a few times to distribute the oil before reinserting the plug.

4. Drain the oil from the crankcase.

5. Replace the air filter and possibly the spark plugs (check your manual).

6. Finally, clean the underside and blades thoroughly and spray them with a lubricating oil or solution to prevent rusting or dirt buildup.

BUYING BY THE "YARD"—Mulch, Sand, Topsoil

Many items bought for home and yard use are sold by the cubic yard. Here's how to calculate how much you'll need:

1. Find the volume of the area to be covered: multiply depth by length by width. The result is the volume in cubic feet.

2. Divide your result by the number of cubic feet in a cubic yard (27).

Example: You want enough mulch to cover an area 10 feet long by 12 feet wide to a depth of 6 inches (or ½ foot).
10 × 12 × .5 = 60 cubic feet
60 ÷ 27 = 2.22 cubic yards

Thickness of Mulch Needed to Control Weeds

Material	Thickness (in)
Compost	2–4
Grass clippings	2–3
Hay	6–8
Leaves (shredded)	2–3
Peat moss	1–2
Pine bark chips	3–4
Pine needles	3–4
Newspapers (shredded)	½–2
Straw	6–8

Super Stain Removal

Fear stains no more! With a few basic supplies and a little patience, you can master the art of stain removal. This alphabetical guide tells the safest, easiest, and most effective ways to get the most common stains out of fabric and other materials in and around the house, including wood, masonry, tile, vinyl, and wallpaper.

Before working on a particular stain, look for any specific or alternative directions for stain removal on any instructions or packaging you still have for the stained material.

The first guideline when you attempt to remove any type of stain from any kind of material is to accept that you may not be able to get rid of the stain completely. The second guideline is not to give up after the first try—repeated efforts often do the trick.

It's smart to keep household stocks of the agents most widely used for removing stains. Have one or two products from each of these categories:

■ **Absorbents** (talcum powder, cornmeal, cornstarch, powdered chalk, fuller's earth, and whiting): soak up stains

■ **Acetone:** dissolves cements and glues; not safe for most synthetic fabrics

■ **Alcohol** (rubbing or denatured): removes many kinds of grime easily and dries quickly

■ **Alkalies** (ammonia, soap, and lye): clean and neutralize acids

■ **Bleaches** (in descending order of strength: chlorine, ammonia, hydrogen peroxide, lemon juice, and white vinegar): clean well and remove discoloration

■ **Detergents:** break up grease; liquid dish detergent is generally safer and more effective than laundry or dishwasher detergent for removing stains

■ **Dry-cleaning solvents** (commonly called cleaning fluids or all-purpose spray cleaners): clean grease, grime, and oil stains

■ **Enzyme products** (enzymatic laundry detergents, pepsin, papain, and mylase): remove complex, protein-laden grease, grime, or oil stains; stronger than standard detergents and dry-cleaning solvents

■ **Paint remover** (turpentine): removes paint, shellac, varnish, and many other stains

Acid (such as battery acid)

Spot wash the stain as soon as possible, using a dab of a paste made of laundry detergent and a little water. Neutralize with ammonia or baking soda paste. Flush with water. If the item is a washable **fabric**, wash as usual.

Asphalt and Tar

Scrape off as much as you can without hurting the material. Soften the remainder by working in petroleum jelly or lard. Sponge with paint remover, being careful not to go outside the stain (or it may spread), and blot with a clean cloth. Repeat this process as necessary until the stain is gone. Do not wash the item if any stain remains or it may spread.

Blood

If **fresh**, sponge it up with cold water. Apply a paste made with water and an enzyme product. Spot wash (or, if **fabric**, wash the entire item) in cold water. Repeat if necessary.

If **dried**, saturate it with cold, soapy water. Let stand for a few minutes and rinse. Saturate it again in cold water with ammonia (3 tablespoons of ammonia per gallon of water). Let stand for a few minutes and flush with a solution of cold water and enzyme product (1 teaspoon enzyme product per

cup of water). Rinse.

If that doesn't work for a **fabric** item, try soaking it for at least 10 hours in cold salt water (2 cups salt per gallon of water), then bleaching (if possible). Wash afterward in cold water.

If that doesn't work on **masonry**, apply a paste of whiting and mineral spirits (both available at hardware stores), let stand, then scrub and flush with cold water.

Catsup

Remove as much as possible (without scraping it into the fabric or driving it further into the wood or masonry). If dry, soften it with water. Then, if **fabric**, flush it with dry-cleaning solvent and wash. If **other material**, gently scrub it with solvent and flush with solvent.

Chewing Gum

If practical, put the item in the freezer for an hour or two so the gum can harden. If not, harden the gum with ice. Then crack the gum with a blunt instrument and scrape off as much as you can. Put a pad of dry-cleaning solvent over the rest and apply pressure. Blot several times, then put a fresh section of solvent-laden pad over the gum and repeat the process. Finally, flush it with solvent and wash.

Coffee

Saturate (or soak) it in a solution of water and liquid detergent. Let stand for 15 minutes without drying. Rinse it and blot with alcohol several times. If **fabric** and the stain remains, stretch the stained part over an open pot and tie it in place with string. Then, from a height of 3 feet, pour boiling water through the stain into the pot. Pour slowly to avoid splashing.

Cosmetics

Sponge it with dry-cleaning solvent, being careful not to go outside the stained area (or the spot may spread). While the stain is still saturated, cover it with a solvent-laden pad and blot. Repeat this process with a fresh pad several times. Then flush with solvent and, if necessary, repeat the entire process until the stain is gone. If **fabric**, wash as usual and, if necessary and safe, bleach.

Crayon: *see* Cosmetics

Dye

On **white fabric**, **bare wood**, or **unpainted masonry**, rub/scrub bleach into the stained area only (to avoid spreading the stain). On **colored fabrics** and **painted materials**, rub/scrub in liquid detergent. Spot wash with warm water and rinse. Then soak the stain in warm water with a splash of vinegar for an hour. Rinse. If the stain is still there, blot it repeatedly with an alcohol and ammonia mixture. Allow 2 or 3 minutes between each blot. Flush with water and, if **fabric**, wash as usual.

Felt-tip Marker: *see* Cosmetics

Fingernail Polish and Remover

If the material is strong enough (many synthetic fabrics aren't), rub/scrub with acetone. If not, rub or scrub with dry-cleaning solvent. Flush with dry-cleaning solvent and repeat if necessary.

Floor Wax

Saturate the stained area with dry-cleaning solvent. Then apply a pad soaked in solvent and blot several times, using a clean pad each time. Flush with solvent. Rub and scrub in liquid detergent with a few drops of ammonia. Blot several times. Flush with water and, if **fabric**, wash in cold water.

Food Coloring

Rub and scrub well with a solution of alcohol and water, plus a splash of vinegar. Flush with water. If the stain persists, apply liquid detergent and blot with a clean pad several times at 2 to 3 minute intervals. Rinse with water and, if **fabric**, wash in cold water.

Fruit

Soak or saturate for a half hour in a mixture of water, liquid detergent, and vinegar (1 quart to 1 teaspoon to 1 tablespoon). Flush with water. If **fabric** and the stain remains, spread the stained area over an open pot, tying the fabric in place with a string. From a height of 3 feet, pour boiling water slowly (to prevent splashing) through the stain into the pot. Wash in cold water.

Glue (airplane)

The only possibility is to apply acetone (note that it can easily dissolve most synthetic fabrics). Flush with dry-cleaning solvent and wash.

Glue (nonepoxy)

There are two possibilities. Apply acetone (which dissolves most synthetic fabrics), flush with dry-cleaning solvent, and wash. Or try the following: Soak or saturate the stained area in a mixture of hot water, liquid detergent, and a splash of vinegar and then flush with water. It may be necessary to soak or saturate the material for up to an hour or to repeat the entire process several times.

Grass

Rub and scrub well with dry-cleaning solvent. Flush with solvent. Sponge and blot with alcohol mixed with a few drops of vinegar. Rinse in water. If the stain persists, repeat the entire process (or, if safe for the material, apply bleach and rinse). If **fabric**, wash as usual.

Grease and Oil (food or organic source)

From **fabric**, scrape away as much as you can. Saturate it with water and rub in enzyme product. Let it set for awhile, making sure it stays moist. Wash in water with liquid detergent.

From **most other materials**, wet the area with alcohol. Then, using a pad soaked in alcohol, rub gently and blot. Repeat several times, using a clean pad each time. If the stain persists, saturate the area with dry-cleaning solvent. Let it stand for several minutes. Then apply a pad soaked in dry-cleaning solvent and blot firmly. Repeat the blotting several times, each time with a clean pad. Wash off the solvent with warm water.

Grease and Oil (machine or mineral source)

For **fabric**, saturate the stained area with dry-cleaning solvent.

Apply a pad soaked in dry-cleaning solvent and blot. Repeat the blotting with a clean pad each time. Flush with water and wash.

To remove a stain from **masonry**, apply a thick paste of mineral spirits and whiting (both available at hardware stores). Allow it to dry and brush it off. Repeat if necessary.

Ink

For **materials other than synthetic fabrics**, rub with acetone.

For **synthetic fabrics**, rub in dry-cleaning solvent. Then saturate a pad in vinegar, apply it to the stain, and blot, pressing firmly. Blot several more times, using a clean pad each time. Flush with dry-cleaning solvent. Repeat if necessary.

Lacquer

The only possible way to remove a lacquer stain is to rub/scrub in acetone, which is not safe for many synthetic fabrics.

Mildew

For **fabric**, brush off as much mildew as possible. Wash in warm water and detergent with a little bleach. Rinse. While still wet, saturate the stain with lemon juice. Let it dry in direct sunlight.

For **most other materials**, brush away all the mildew you can. Then saturate the stained area with a 50/50 solution of water and bleach. Let stand for an hour, then scrub with the same solution. Rinse with water. Repeat if necessary. Warning: Be careful not to get the bleach mixture on grass or plantings. If it would be difficult to avoid doing so, use straight vinegar instead of the bleach solution.

Milk

Apply a thick paste made with water and enzyme product to the stained area. Let it set for about 20 minutes without allowing it to dry. Flush with water and, if **fabric**, wash.

Mustard: *see* Catsup

Oil: *see* Grease and Oil

Paint (latex or water-based)

If **wet**, remove as much as possible by gently blotting or scraping, then spot-wash stained area with water and liquid detergent.

If **dry**, apply paint remover to moisten the paint (which may require a lengthy period of soaking) before following the above procedure.

Paint (alkyd or oil-based)

After removing any paint that's wet, saturate the stained area with paint remover and allow it to set for several minutes. Gently remove liquefied paint and repeat the process until the stain is gone.

Perspiration

Soak the fabric or other material for 45 minutes in a solution of 1 quart warm water, 1 teaspoon liquid detergent, and 1½ tablespoons ammonia. Rinse. Saturate stained area with vinegar and soak for another 45 minutes in warm water. Rinse and, if **fabric**, wash as usual.

Putty

Gently lift or scrape off as much as possible. Then soak/saturate the stained area with dry-cleaning solvent and let stand several minutes. Apply a pad soaked in solvent and blot, pressing firmly. Blot several times, using a clean pad each time. Flush with solvent. Repeat the entire process if necessary.

Rust

To remove rust from **fabric**, rub into the stain a thick paste of salt and vinegar (add lemon juice if the fabric is all cotton). Let stand for 45 minutes. Flush with water and repeat if necessary. When finished, flush with water and wash as usual.

For **most other materials**, use rust remover (available from hardware stores) as directed.

Shellac

Saturate or soak the stained area with dry-cleaning solvent. Apply a pad soaked in solvent and blot firmly. Repeat the blotting several times, each time with a clean pad. Then saturate or soak the area with alcohol and blot several times with dry pad. Flush with alcohol. Repeat the entire process if necessary, then, if **fabric**, wash in cold water.

Smoke and Soot

For **fabric** and **most nonmasonry materials**, saturate the stained area with dry-cleaning solvent. Apply a pad soaked in solvent and blot firmly. Repeat the blotting, each time with a clean pad. Flush with solvent, then saturate the stained area with a mix of liquid detergent and a few drops of ammonia. Let stand for a couple minutes, then blot with dry pad. Rinse thoroughly with water. If fabric, wash as usual.

If the stain is on **wood, plaster**, or **wallpaper**, you may have to paint or paper over the stained area, even if the stain is removed, to eliminate the smell.

To remove smoke and soot from **masonry**, apply a thick paste of whiting and mineral spirits (both available at hardware stores). Allow it to dry and brush it off. Repeat if necessary. If the stain is heavy or if you suspect the presence of creosote (for example, on a wood-burning chimney), you may have to cover the stain with an aluminum sealer and one or more coats of paint.

Tar: *see* Asphalt and Tar

Tea: *see* Coffee

Urine

Soak or saturate the stained area for 45 minutes in a mix of warm water and liquid detergent with a splash of ammonia. Then rub in vinegar (or lemon juice, except with synthetic fabrics). Blot with a cloth and rinse with warm water. Then cover the stain with a liquid enzyme product (or a paste of enzyme product and warm water). If **fabric**, wash as usual. If **other material**, spot-wash and rinse with warm water.

Varnish

Flush the stained area with dry-cleaning solvent. Blot dry. If the material is strong enough (most synthetic fabrics aren't), saturate the stained area with acetone or paint remover. If not, use solvent. Then apply a pad soaked in the same substance and blot, pressing firmly. Blot several times, using a clean pad each time. Flush with solvent. If **fabric**, wash as usual. If **other material**, rinse with water.

Vomit

Remove as much as you can with a wet cloth (warm water). Rub enzyme product into the stained area (if the product is dry, first make it into a paste with warm water). Then soak or saturate the area in a solution of warm water and liquid detergent with a splash of ammonia. Let stand for 30 minutes and flush with water. If **fabric**, wash as usual.

Water

For **fabric** and **most nonmasonry materials**, apply a thick paste of lemon juice (or, if synthetic fabric, vinegar) and salt to the stained area itself, avoiding as much nonstained area as you can. Let stand 15 minutes. Gently scrub, rinse, and blot dry.

To remove from **masonry**, apply a thick paste of mineral spirits and whiting (both available at hardware stores) to the stained area. Allow it to dry and brush it off.

Wax (automobile)

Soak or saturate the stained area with dry-cleaning solvent. Cover it with clean cloth padding (if **loose fabric**, such as clothing, cover both sides with padding). Blot several times, increasing pressure each time. Repeat the process with a clean pad. Continue until the stain is removed.

Wax (candle)

To remove wax from **fabric**, scrape off as much as you can without damaging the fabric. (If practical, you may want to put the fabric in the freezer for several hours before scraping. Sometimes this hardens the wax so that it all scrapes off easily). Then try one or both of the following:

• Stretch the stained area over the top of a big pot and secure it in place with a string. From 3 feet above the pot, pour boiling water slowly (to avoid splashing) through the stain into the pot.

• On a flat surface suitable for ironing, place the stained area between two layers of paper towels. Then iron over the stain so the wax melts into the towels. Move the towels each time you iron to provide a fresh blotter.

To clear any remaining stain, try soaking it in lemon juice or (if safe for the fabric) some stronger bleach. Then flush with water and wash in cold water.

To remove wax from most **other materials**, harden the wax as much as possible with ice, then scrape off as much as you can without driving the wax further into the material. Place a thin cloth rag over the stain and iron over it so that the wax melts into the cloth. Repeat this process with a clean rag each time you iron.

Wine

From **fabric**, if wet, gently blot up as much as possible, then apply a thick layer of salt. Allow the area to dry, then remove the salt.

If dry, saturate the stained area with cold water to render the wine wet, and follow the above process. Then, if possible, stretch the dry stained area over an open pot and tie the fabric in place with a string. From a height of 3 feet, pour boiling water through the stain and into the pot, slowly to avoid splashing.

If it's not possible to stretch the dry stained area over a pot, saturate the stained area with cold water and, using a pad soaked in liquid detergent, blot the stain firmly several times, each time with a clean pad. Flush with cold water and blot dry, using dry pad.

From **most other materials**, if wet and on a horizontal surface, gently blot up as much as possible, then apply a thick layer of salt. Allow the area to dry. If dry and on a horizontal surface, saturate the stained area with cold water, wait a couple of minutes, and follow the above process. If wet or dry on a nonhorizontal surface, remove as much as possible by blotting with a cloth (a dry cloth on a wet surface, a wet cloth on a dry one).

After any of the above procedures, saturate the stained area with a mixture of water, liquid detergent, and vinegar. Let stand a few minutes and blot. Repeat the saturation and blotting until the stain is removed. Flush with water.

APPENDIX
Home Repair Terms

A

aggregate: sand and stone particles used in mixtures: for example, with cement and water to make concrete; with paint to provide texture or (on floors) traction

airlock: blockage in a pipe created by an air bubble

amp: a measure of the volume of electricity traveling through a circuit at any one time

architrave: molding or frame around the perimeter of a door, window, or arch

B

balustrade: the barrier (wall or hand-rail), sometimes called a **banister**, framing a staircase or landing; each spindle supporting a handrail is called a baluster.

batt: a section of fiberglass or rock-wool insulation that is 4 to 8 feet long

batten: a narrow strip of wood that covers the joint between two boards or panels

beam: a horizontal wooden or metal piece that supports a floor or roof

bearing wall: a wall that is critical to the support of a roof or floor

blanket: a section of fiberglass or rock-wool insulation that is more than 8 feet long

blocking: a horizontal piece of wood between studs

bond: the pattern in which bricks, paving stones, or masonry blocks are laid; or the adhesion created by a glue or cement

bore: (n) the hollow interior of a pipe or tube; (v) to drill

BTU (British Thermal Unit): a rating unit for heating and cooling equipment, 1 BTU being the amount of heat required to raise the temperature of 1 pound of water by 1 degree Fahrenheit

burr: a rough edge created by sawing or filing a piece of wood

butt hinge: the type of simple, swinging hinge most frequently used on doors, with one leaf mounted on the door itself and the other on the jamb

C

cap-nut: a nut used to tighten a pipe fitting

casing: wooden molding around a door or window

caulk: (n) any compound used to seal cracks, seams, gaps, or leaks; (v) to apply such a compound

cement: a powdery binder that mixes with water and aggregate to form concete

CFM (cubic feet per minute): a measure used in heating and cooling equipment to refer to air movement capability

chalk (or chalking): the powdery residue left by eroding paint

chase: (n) a groove in masonry or plaster to accomodate a pipe, cable, or wire; (v) to make this kind of groove

circuit: the entire electrical path through which a current flows

circuit breaker: a switch that enables you to shut off electrical current in the event of a short circuit, an overload, or the need to do electrical work in safety

concave: a curve that goes inward (away from viewer); the opposite of convex

concrete: masonry material made by mixing water, aggregate, and cement

condensing unit: the outdoor part of an air conditioner or cooling system that gives off heat

conductor: a medium through which electricity flows (most commonly referring to a wire)

convection: the current creating by rising hot air

convex: a curve that goes outward (toward the viewer); the opposite of concave

cornice: molding between a wall and a ceiling

counterbore: (n) a wider hole on top of a bore that enables the head of a screw or bolt to lie below the surface; (v) to create such a hole

countersink: (n) a tapered hole on top of a bore that enables the head of a screw or bolt to lie flush with the surface; (v) to create such a hole

course: one parallel layer of bricks, singles, or horizontal boards or siding

cup: a bend across a piece of wood caused by shrinkage

D

dado: a cross-grain groove in a piece of wood

damper: a valve-flap in a chimney that can be adjusted to facilitate or impede the flow of air and smoke

damp-proof course (DPC): a layer of material that blocks moisture, also referred to as a **damp-proof membrane (DPM)**

dead-bolt lock: a lock that, when in place, can be turned only with a key on the outside or by hand on the inside

double-cylinder lock: a lock that, when in place, can be turned only with a key on either side

drop: a strip of wallpaper that's cut and ready for pasting

drywall: a prefabricated building material that comes in sheets and is used in place of a plastered wall (sometimes called plasterboard, gypsum board, or wallboard)

E

eave: an edge of the roof that extends beyond the wall

efflorescence: a powderlike deposit that forms on masonry as a result of interior salts rising to the surface

elbow: a pipe or conduit fitting that enables you to switch directions

end grain: exposed wood at the end of a plank or beam or alongside a cut

F

fascia board: horizontal wooden strip covering a rafter, support beam, or top of an exterior wall, such as the strip to which a gutter may be fastened

feather: to smooth or obscure an unwanted edge (such as the edge of a plaster patch) so that it's less visible

female part: a nut or fitting into which another part (called male) is inserted

flashing: a strip of metal or shingle weatherproofing between two roof surfaces, a roof and a chimney, or a roof and a wall

flue: any chimney, pipe, or duct that transports smoke and gases to the outside

footing: a masonry foundation for a wall

frost line: the lowest depth to which the ground can freeze in a given area (footings must extend a bit beyond this depth.)

fuse box: houses fuses that mediate between the main electrical cable coming into the house and the various electrical circuits within the house

G

galvanized: protected by a layer of zinc

glazing: the process of installing new glass, usually involving the use of glazing compound (an adhesive) and glazier's points (brackets to hold glass in place)

grade: the ground level (elevation and slope) of a given area

grain: the direction of fibers within a piece of wood, visible as alternating light and dark streaks

grommet: rubber or plastic lining in a hole to safeguard an interior wire or cable

ground: in electricity, a neutral wire that carries current safely into the earth and/or protects against shock

gypsum board: *see* drywall

H

hardboard: a prefabricated sheet of construction material that incorporates wooden fibers

hardwood: wood from deciduous (nonevergreen) trees; most durable for building; cleanest and most heat-producing for burning

heave: a swelling in the ground caused by moisture (often frost)

hone: to sharpen a blade

I

insulation: in heating and cooling, any material that serves as a buffer between hot and cold air; in electricity, any material that protects wires or cables and prevents shock; otherwise, any material that reduces sound transmission

J

jamb: a vertical side piece framing a door or window

joint compound: a filler used in conjunction with tape to cover and hide joints between drywall sheets

joist: a horizontal beam supporting a floor, ceiling, or wall

K

kilowatt: in electricity, 1,000 watts; household electrical use is commonly based on the number of kilowatts consumed in an hour

L

laminate: to bond two or more layers of material, such as wood or plastic

lath: strip of wood nailed to wall studs or joists that is meant to underlie plaster

lintel: horizontal beam over a door or window

M

male part: any bolt or part that fits inside another part (called female)

mastic: substance that seals joints without setting

miter: (n) a joint that features two pieces of wood whose meeting ends have been cut at corresponding angles; (v) to make such a cut; a **miter box** is a sawing aid that holds a piece of wood and guides the saw to cut it at any one of a variety of common angles

mortise: a cut in a piece of wood designed to hold another piece of wood

mullion: a vertical divider in a window frame

N

neutral: in an electrical circuit, that part that is not "live," that is not transmitting current to its outlet; the opposite of positive

newel: the top or bottom stair post supporting a handrail

O

oxidize: to rust

P

panel: any piece of material, wooden or otherwise, that is set into a frame; or any single, rectangular unit of construction material, such as drywall, hardboard, or plywood

pier: a masonry post or support

pilot hole: a small hole drilled or nailed before a screw is installed, to guide it and provide easier entry

plasterboard: *see* drywall

plumb: absolutely vertical (90-degree angle to the horizon); also any tool that helps you determine plumb

plywood: a prefabricated sheet of building material made by laminating together several layers of wood

positive: in an electrical circuit, the part that is "live" or "hot," that transmits current to its outlet; the opposite of neutral or ground

pressure-treated wood: wood that has been infused with a preservative to guard against rot

primer: the paint that is used to make a first sealing coat over a bare surface, prior to the application of subsequent coats of paint containing the desired pigment

PVC (polyvinyl chloride): plastic pipe or tubing

R

R-value: a measure of insulation, based on the resistance offered to heat transfer: the higher the R-value, the stronger the insulation

rafter: sloping beam that supports a roof

ratchet: a device (such as an automobile tire jack or socket wrench) that facilitates movement in one direction only by using a toothed-wheel that prevents reverse movement

retaining wall: a wall that supports a slope in the ground and thereby helps prevent erosion

riser: the vertical piece in a stair step

S

sash: the part of a window that opens and shuts

settling/settlement: the periodic shifting of a house or structure in the ground, most commonly caused by freeze-thaw cycles

sheath (or sheathing): in electricity, the outer layer of insulation protecting a cable or wire

shim: a thin layer of wood or some other material used as an insert to make a better fitting adjustment

short circuit: an interruption in the electrical circuit that shortens it, intensifies the current, and therefore can easily blow a fuse

sill: the lowest horizontal piece in a door frame, window frame, or wall partition

soffit: the underside of an eave

softwood: wood from evergreen trees; easier to cut but less durable than hardwood; quicker to burn but not as hot- or clean-burning

soil pipe: the pipe that transports waste material from the house to the sewer or septic system

strike: the metal plate on a door jamb that facilitates the operation of a lock

stud: a vertical piece of lumber in a wood-framed wall

T

template: a cut-out pattern (usually actual size) that serves as a guide in shaping something

tenon: the part of a piece of wood that fits into a mortise cut into another piece of wood

terminal: in electricity, the end-point connection for an electrical wire or conductor

thinner: a solution used to dilute or liquefy paint, stain, or varnish

torque: the force of rotation

transom: a horizontal divider in a window frame

trap: a dipped section of pipe immediately below a sink that collects otherwise troublesome debris and, because of its standing water, blocks gases traveling through the plumbing system

tread: the horizontal surface on a stair step

V

vapor barrier (or vapor check): a layer of material in a floor, wall, or ceiling that blocks moisture from the air

volt: in electricity, a measure of pressure

W

wallboard: *see* drywall

water hammer: a vibration, often noisy, caused by shifting levels of water pressure

watt: in electricity, a measure of the amount of power consumed:
volts × amps = watts

weep hole: a small hole created at the bottom of a wall to drain out trapped moisture

APPENDIX

Do-It-Yourself Charts and Calculations

"Measure twice, cut once" is a standard piece of advice from experienced carpenters. They have learned to always double check their measurements and pencil marks before picking up the saw. The lesson is quickly learned when a piece of expensive material is ruined by cutting it to 46 inches when it should have been 48 inches.

With that in mind, use the following tables and charts to find all the home improvement numbers you might need. These charts, tables, and formulas will save you lots of time and guesswork before, during, and after many home improvements.

Which Home Improvements Pay Off?

Improvement	% Return on Investment Upon House Sale
Kitchen remodeling (major)	90–100
Kitchen remodeling (minor)	85
Bath—add second full	85
Bath remodeling	75
Master suite—add	80
Sun room—add	60
Family room with fireplace—add	80
New exterior siding	75
New windows	55–60
New doors	40
Deck or patio	50–70
Swimming pool	30

HOW LONG WILL IT LAST?

The estimates given assume normal use, good initial product quality, and careful upkeep (and in the case of wallpaper and paint, careful surface preparation).

Wallpaper: 10 years

Interior Paint: 5 years

Exterior Paint: 8 years

An unopened can of oil-based (alklyd) paint can last up to 50 years, but an unopened can of water-based (latex) paint may be good for only 7 or 8 years.

RULES OF THUMB: BUYING WALLPAPER

After using the table at right to get a general estimate of rolls of wallpaper needed, you can refine your estimate by doing the following:

■ Subtract 1 single roll for every two windows or one door in the room.
■ Subtract 1 or 2 single rolls for a kitchen with many cabinets.
■ Add 1 or 2 single rolls for patterns that have wide matches (called "pattern repeat" and given in inches on the label or in the wallpaper book).

One other number is important when buying wallpaper: the "run" number. Be sure before you start that all rolls have come from the same run, as marked on each roll's label. Rolls that were printed at different times (meaning different runs) may have slight color variations.

Estimating Rolls of Wallpaper Needed

Wallpaper usually comes packaged in two-roll bolts but is priced by the single roll. The average roll contains about 30 square feet; the width of a roll can vary.

Ceiling Height

Size of Room (ft)	8 ft	9 ft	10 ft	11 ft	12 ft	Border Needed (yds)
			Single Rolls Needed			
5 x 6	8	8	10	11	12	11
8 x 10	9	10	11	12	13	13
10 x 10	10	11	13	14	15	15
10 x 12	11	12	14	15	16	16
10 x 14	12	14	15	16	18	17
12 x 12	12	14	15	16	18	17
12 x 14	13	15	16	18	19	18
12 x 16	14	16	17	19	21	20
12 x 18	15	17	19	20	22	21
12 x 20	16	18	20	22	24	23
14 x 14	14	16	17	19	21	20
14 x 16	15	17	19	20	22	21
14 x 18	16	18	20	22	24	23
14 x 20	17	19	21	23	25	24
14 x 22	18	20	22	24	27	25
16 x 16	16	18	20	22	24	23
16 x 18	17	19	21	23	25	24
16 x 20	18	20	22	24	27	25
16 x 22	16	21	23	26	28	27
16 x 24	20	22	25	27	30	28
18 x 18	18	20	22	24	27	25
18 x 20	19	21	23	25	28	27
18 x 22	20	22	25	27	30	28
18 x 24	21	23	26	28	31	29

Estimating Gallons of Paint Needed—Interior

Walls

Coverage: 1 gallon of paint can cover anywhere from 350 to 500 square feet, depending on the brand of paint and the condition of the surface. We use 350 square feet in the calculations below to provide a conservative estimate.

1. To calculate square feet, add the lengths of each wall and multiply your total by the ceiling height.
> *Example:* A 12 by 20 foot room that has 8-foot ceilings would be
> 12 + 12 + 20 + 20 = 64 x 8 = 512 square feet.

2. From that figure, subtract 20 square feet for each door and fireplace and 15 square feet for each window.
> *Example:* 1 door = 20 square feet, 3 windows = 45 square feet, for a total of 65 square feet.
> 512 - 65 = 447 square feet

3. Divide your result by 350.
> *Example:* 447 ÷ 350 = 1.277 gallons of paint

There are 4 quarts in a gallon, so you could buy 1 gallon and 2 quarts, although 2 quarts may cost almost as much as a gallon; check prices before you decide.

4. If you need to apply two coats, double the number of quarts or gallons.

Ceiling

Using wall or ceiling paint, which covers about 350 square feet, multiply the length by the width of the room to get total square feet.
> *Example:* For a 12 by 20 room, 12 x 20 = 240 square feet.

You would need a gallon of paint for one coat.

Trim

Trim paints cover between 350 and 400 square feet per gallon, or between 80 and 100 square feet per quart.

1. Allow 8 square feet for each window and 25 square feet for each door.
> *Example:* 1 door = 25 square feet, 3 windows = 24 square feet, for a total of 49 square feet.

For window trim and the door, you would need 1 quart of trim paint.

2. To calculate base, chair rail, and ceiling molding, measure their length in inches and multiply by 6. Then divide that figure by 144 to get the number of square feet.
> *Example:* For a 12 by 20 foot room with base and ceiling moldings,
> 12 + 12 + 20 + 20 = 64 feet x 12 = 768 inches x 6 = 4,608;
> 4,608 x 2 (base and ceiling moldings) = 9,216;
> 9,216 ÷ 144 = 64 square feet.

For the moldings, you would need 1 quart of trim paint.

Estimating Gallons of Paint Needed—Exterior

To calculate how much paint you will need for the exterior of your house, do the following:

Walls

1. Measure the length of each outside wall and add together. Then multiply by the height to the gables.

Example: Your two-story house is a rectangle 20 feet deep and 50 feet wide, so 20 + 20 + 50 + 50 = 140 x 18 feet high = 2,520 square feet.

2. To calculate the area of the gables, multiply one-half their width by their height and multiply by the number of gables.

Example: This house has two gables, 10 feet high, and 50 feet wide, so 25 x 10 x 2 = 500 square feet.

3. Add the results of steps 1 and 2, in this example,
2,520 + 500 = 3,020.

4. Divide that number by 400 (or the amount of coverage shown on the can label) to determine number of gallons needed:
3,020 ÷ 400 = 7.55 gallons.

Trim

To figure trim paint needed, count all windows and multiply by 15 square feet, and count all doors and multiply by 20 square feet.

Example: 10 windows x 15 = 150 square feet, 2 doors x 20 = 40 square feet, for a total of 190 square feet or about ½ gallon (2 quarts) of trim paint.

Coverage Capacity of Various Finishes

Product	Square Feet per Gallon
Lacquer	200–300
Lacquer sealer	250–300
Paint	350–650
Shellac	300–350
Stain, oil-based	300–350
Stain, water-based	350–400
Varnish	300–350
Wax, liquid	600–700
Wax, paste	125–175

Light-Reflecting Power of Paint Colors

The color of your interior walls can affect the amount of reflective light available in a room; the greater the percentage of light-reflecting power, the better the visibility for close work such as reading and crafts.

Color	% of Light Reflected
White	70–90
Cream, ivory	55–90
Light yellow	65–70
Light green	40–50
Medium green	15–30
Medium gray	15–30
Orange	15–30
Medium blue	15–20
Dark blue	5–10
Red, maroon	3–18
Medium dark brown	3–18

Quick Calculations to Determine Board Feet

Lumber Size (in)	To Get Board Feet—
1 x 4	Divide linear length by 3
1 x 6	Divide linear length by 2
1 x 8	Multiply linear length by 0.66
1 x 12	Linear length equals board feet
2 x 4	Multiply linear length by 0.66
2 x 6	Linear length equals board feet
2 x 8	Multiply linear length by 1.33
2 x 12	Multiply linear length by 2

Standard Sizes—Interior Materials

Item	Standard Width(s)	Standard Height(s)/Length(s)
Doors		
Bathroom, closet	24"–30"	6'8"
Bifold (2-door)	2', 2'8", 3'	6'8"
Double-entry	60", 64", 72"	6'8"
Front	36"	6'8"
Garage (double)	16'	6½', 7'
Garage (single)	9'	6½', 7'
Louvered	1'3"–3'	6'8"
Room	30"	6'8"
Sliding glass	60", 72"	80"
Windows		
Bay	6'–12'	3½'–7'
Bow	6'–15'	3'–7'
Sash	20"–40"	34"–64"
Sliding glass	36", 48"	24", 34", 48", 56"
Bathroom Fixtures		
Bathtub	2', 2'6"–2'8"	4'6", 5', 5'6"
Shower stall	2'6"–3'6"	2'6"–3'6"
Sink	30"–40"	22"
Toilet	19"–20"	26" (depth)
Kitchen Equipment		
Dishwasher	24"	24¼"–30" (depth)
Range/oven	30"–36"	23½"–25" (depth)
Refrigerator	28"–35"	25"–30" (depth)
Sink (double)	32"	20" (depth)
Sink (single)	24", 30"	21" (depth)

Weight of Common Substances

Substance	Approximate Weight (lbs/cubic ft)
Book (hardback)	30–40
Brick, common	125
Clothing (firmly packed)	10–15
Concrete	145
Earth (moist, loose)	70–80
Gasoline	45–50
Gold	1,204
Iron (cast)	450
Lead	710
Mud	110–130
Oil	55–60
Sand	90–120
Silver	655
Snow (compacted)	15–50
Steel	490
Stone	160 (can vary)
Water (1 gal = 8.336 lbs)	62.4 (7½ gal)

Mortar Requirements

Here's the formula for making 1 cubic foot of general-use mortar:

Mix together

- 16 pounds Portland cement
- 8½ pounds hydrated lime
- 100 pounds dry sand
- 2 to 3 gallons water

Mortar Required for Common Brick (8" x 3¾" x 2¼")

Joint Thickness (in)	Cubic feet of mortar per 1,000 bricks
¼	9
⅜	14
½	20

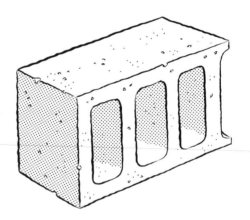

Thickness Needed for Various Types of Insulation to Obtain R-Value

The R-value measures a material's ability to resist heat conduction. The higher the R-value, the better a material's insulating ability. It is defined as:

$$\frac{\textit{temperature difference} \times \textit{area} \times \textit{time}}{\textit{heat loss}}$$

Inches of Thickness Needed: Loose and Blown Fill

R-Value	Mineral Fiber Blanket or Batts	Fiberglass	Rock Wool	Cellulosic Fiber	Perlite or Vermiculite
R-11	3¼–3¾	4–5¼	3½	3¾	3–4½
R-19*	5¾–6¼	7–8¾	6¼	6½	5½–7¾
R-30	9–9½	11–14	9¾	10½	8½–12¼
R-38	11½–12	14–17¾	12¼–13	10½–15½	
R-49	15–15½	18–23	16	17	13¾–20

Source: U.S. Department of Energy

Note: Rigid cellular insulating boards have R-values of 4 to 8, depending on type, for 1 inch of thickness.

** See sidebar, below.*

R-Value: Thickness Needed to Meet Recommended Standard of R-19 for Exterior Walls

Material	Thickness (in)
Brick	96
Concrete blocks	72
Wallboard	24
½" Plywood	18
Urethane foam	3

U.S. DEPARTMENT of ENERGY INSULATION ZONES

Recommended R-Values for Existing Houses in Eight Insulation Zones[a]

Component	Ceilings Below Ventilated Attics		Floors Over Unheated Crawl spaces, Basements	
Insulation Zone	Oil, Gas, Heat Pump	Electric Resistance	Oil, Gas, Heat Pump	Electric Resistance
1	19	30	0	0
2	30	30	0	0
3	30	38	0	19
4	30	38	19	19
5	38	38	19	19
6	38	38	19	19
7	38	49	19	19
8	49	49	19	19

Component	Exterior Wallsb (Wood Frame)		Crawl space Wallsc	
Insulation Zone	Oil, Gas, Heat Pump	Electric Resistance	Oil, Gas, Heat Pump	Electric Resistance
1	0	11	11	11
2	11	11	19	19
3	11	11	19	19
4	11	11	19	19
5	11	11	19	19
6	11	11	19	19
7	11	11	19	19
8	11	11	19	19

Source: U.S. Department of Energy

a. These recommendations are based on the assumption that no structural modifications are needed to accommodate the added insulation.

b. R-value of full wall insulation, which is 32 inches thick, will depend on material used. Range is R-11 to R-13. For new construction, R-19 is recommended for exterior walls. Jamming an R-19 batt in a 32-inch cavity will not yield R-19.

c. Insulate crawl space walls only if the crawl space is dry all year, the floor above is not insulated, and all ventilation to the crawl space is blocked. A vapor barrier (e.g., 4- or 6-mil polyethylene film) should be installed on the ground to reduce moisture migration into the crawl space.

Sizing Ceiling Fans

Room Size (ft)	Minimum Fan Diameter (in)
10 x 10	36
10 x 15	42
12 x 14	42
12 x 18	48

Appliance Life Expectancy

Appliance	Average Life Expectancy (yrs)
Air conditioner (central)	15
Air conditioner (room)	12
Blender	10
Clothes dryer	14–18
Clothes washer	11–13
Coffee maker (drip)	6–8
Color television	8–12
Dishwasher	11–13
Food processor	8–10
Freezer	15–20
Furnace	25–30
Microwave oven	10–12
Range/oven	16–20
Refrigerator/freezer	16–20
Water heater	10–12
Vacuum cleaner	15

Comparing Lightbulb Brightness

The brightness of a lightbulb is measured in lumens (equal to 1 standard candle); energy consumed is measured in watts. Here are some general equivalents (brands may vary):

Watts	Lumens
15	125
25	215
40	480–510
60	880
75	855–1,210
100	1,600–1,750
150	2,790

Comparing Types of LightBulbs

Bulb Type	Lumens per Watt	Life (hrs)
Incandescent	14–18	750–1,000+
Fluorescent tube	up to 105	6,000–20,000
Compact fluorescent	up to 105	10,000
Halogen	15–22	2,500–3,500

INCANDESCENT BULB

Electrical Measurement

Unit	Multiple	Value
volt	kilovolt (kV)	1,000 volts
volt	millivolt (mV)	1/1,000 volt
volt	microvolt (μV)	1/1,000,000 volt
ohm	kilohm (kΩ)	1,000 ohms
ohm	megohm (MΩ)	1,000,000 ohms
ampere	milliampere (mA)	1/1,000 ampere
ampere	microampere (μA)	1/1,000,000 ampere

The original unit of quantity was the coulomb, which was equal to the passage of 6¼ times 10^{18} electrons past a point in the electrical system.

The ampere is the unit of electrical flow; it is equal to the flow of 1 coulomb per second. The amp is the basic unit for electricity in the International System.

The volt measures electrical potential energy, which is 1 joule per coulomb.

The watt, equal to 1 joule per second, is the basic unit for measuring electrical power. One kilowatt equals 1,000 watts.

The ohm is the unit for measuring electrical resistance, which is the resistance a circuit offers to the flow of 1 ampere driven by the force of 1 volt.

MULTI TESTER
FOR ELECTRICAL MEASUREMENTS

APPENDIX
Organizations and Services

Energy Conservation Center
Public Service Electric and Gas Company
P.O. Box 1258
Newark, NJ 07101
800-854-4444

Specialists can provide information on specific energy needs such as weatherization, appliance efficiency and rebates, and home energy audit publications. The center receives calls weekdays between 9 A.M. and 5 P.M., EST.

Genova Plumbers Hotline
7034 East Court Street
Davison, MI 48423
800-521-7488

The staff can suggest solutions to plumbing problems involving gutters and plastic fittings as well as more technical problems. The hotline operates weekdays between 8 A.M. and 5 P.M., EST.

Major Appliance Consumer Action Panel (MACAP)
20 North Wacker Drive
Chicago, IL 60606
800-621-0477
312-984-5858 (in Illinois, Alaska, Hawaii)
MACAP will respond to written inquiries about problems with major appliances. Call for further instructions. It is open weekdays from 8:30 A.M. to 5 P.M., CST

Shopsmith, Inc.
6530 Poe Avenue
Dayton, OH 45414
800-543-7586

Shopsmith will answer questions related to wood-working. If they cannot answer your question, they will research the information and call back. Call weekdays between 9 A.M. and midnight and Saturdays between 9 A.M. and 6 P.M., EST.

Soap and Detergent Association
475 Park Avenue South
New York, NY 10016
212-725-1262

This association will answer questions on all aspects of soaps and detergents. They also have free publications. Call Monday through Friday from 9 A.M. to 4:45 P.M., EST.

ON-LINE HELP FOR HOME PROJECTS

Computer on-line services such as America Online, Genie, Prodigy, and CompuServe offer subscribers access to electronic bulletin boards, E-mail, and even the editors of several popular home improvement magazines. The address of the True Value Web Site is **www.truevalue.com**; its HOMEWORK section offers helpful advice and projects to do around your house each month.

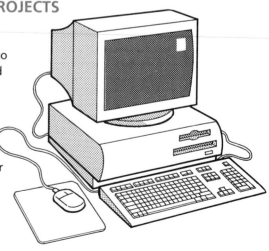

Index

A
acrylic latex caulk, 172
adhesive bonds, 28
adjustable wrench, 20, 118
air-conditioners, 163–66
   life expectancies, 230
alkyd paint, 72, 85, 86, 88
   removal, 208
aluminum furniture, 181
ammonia precaution, 36
annular threaded nails, 14
appliances
   defective, 144
   life expectancies, 230
   plug replacement, 145–46
   safety measures, 142
   smoke or sparks, 139–40
   standard sizes, 224
asbestos shingles, 168
ashes recycling, 188
asphalt shingles, 168, 169, 182
attic moisture, 168, 169

B
baking soda, 37, 106
barbed nails, 14
basement dampness, 69–70
bathtub
   caulking, 132
   showerhead cleaning, 133–34
   standard sizes, 224
   unclogging, 119
bleach, 36, 203
block plane, 28
blower, furnace, 157
bonding primer, 73
bonds, 28, 29–30
broom, 33–34
brushes, paint, 76–77
   cleaning, 84–85, 86
   restoring, 86
butyl caulk, 172

C
cabinet hanging, 66–67
calendar planner, 39–50
carpenter's level, 21
caulking
   bathroom, 132
   house, 48, 89, 166, 171–73

caulking gun, 172–73
C-clamps, 118
ceiling
   fan sizes, 230
   painting, 74, 75, 82, 220
   sagging or leaking, 52–53
cement crack repair, 174–75
central air conditioning, 163–64, 230
ceramic tile replacement, 62–63
chisels, 28
circuit breaker, 139, 141, 143, 144
claw hammers, 13
cleaning, 36–37
   baking soda uses, 37, 106
   caulking gun, 173
   furnace ducts and fan, 157, 158
   garden tools, 201
   outdoor furniture, 180, 181, 182
   paint on hands, 85
   safety measures, 36
   showerhead, 133–34
   stain removal, 203–11
   tools, 33–36
   vegetable oil use, 183
   WD-40 use, 27
clogged drains, 119–22
cloths, cleaning, 34
cola drink, 33
common nails, 14
concrete repair, 174–75, 183
continuity tester, 138
cooling system, 163–66
   economies, 165, 166
cordless power tools, 16, 20
corn straw broom, 33–34
crescent (adjustable) wrench, 20
cross-cut saw, 22
curtain rod mounting, 65
curved claw hammer, 13
cutters, 26

D
deck water seal, 183
deer deterrents, 194
doors, 108–12
   frame cracks or gaps, 171
   lock problems, 100–101
   painting, 84
   sliding, 111–12
   standard sizes, 224
   sticking/sagging, 108–10

ABOUT THE AUTHOR

JACK MAGUIRE has written many books in a variety of fields, including how-to books on home maintenance, landscaping, kids' rooms, spas and hot tubs, and home gyms. He lives in Highland, New York.